Spiritual Warfare Prayers

Bible Verses, Quotes, Prayers, and Study to Help You Get Through Times of Spiritual Darkness

© Copyright 2025 - All rights reserved.

The content contained within this book may not be reproduced, duplicated, or transmitted without direct written permission from the author or the publisher.

Under no circumstances will any blame or legal responsibility be held against the publisher or author for any damages, reparation, or monetary loss due to the information contained within this book, either directly or indirectly.

Legal Notice:

This book is copyright-protected. It is only for personal use. You cannot amend, distribute, sell, use, quote, or paraphrase any part of the content within this book without the consent of the author or publisher.

Disclaimer Notice:

Please note the information contained within this document is for educational and entertainment purposes only. All effort has been executed to present accurate, up-to-date, reliable, and complete information. No warranties of any kind are declared or implied. Readers acknowledge that the author is not engaging in the rendering of legal, financial, medical, or professional advice. The content within this book has been derived from various sources. Please consult a licensed professional before attempting any techniques outlined in this book.

By reading this document, the reader agrees that under no circumstances is the author responsible for any losses, direct or indirect, that are incurred as a result of the use of the information contained within this document, including, but not limited to, errors, omissions, or inaccuracies.

Your Free Gift
(only available for a limited time)

Thanks for getting this book! If you want to learn more about various spirituality topics, then join Mari Silva's community and get a free guided meditation MP3 for awakening your third eye. This guided meditation mp3 is designed to open and strengthen ones third eye so you can experience a higher state of consciousness. Simply visit the link below the image to get started.

https://spiritualityspot.com/meditation

Or, Scan the QR code!

Table of Contents

INTRODUCTION 1
CHAPTER 1: THE BIBLE STUDY OF SPIRITUAL WARFARE 2
CHAPTER 2: THE ARMOR OF GOD: VERSES TO EQUIP YOURSELF
FOR BATTLE..15
CHAPTER 3: PRAYERS FOR STRENGTH IN TIMES OF DARKNESS 24
CHAPTER 4: BIBLE VERSES FOR VICTORY IN WARFARE 35
CHAPTER 5: QUOTES OF FAITH AND ENCOURAGEMENT 45
CHAPTER 6: PRAYERS FOR SPECIFIC SPIRITUAL ATTACKS 54
CHAPTER 7: PRAYERS FOR PROTECTION AND DELIVERANCE 64
CHAPTER 8: LIVING DAILY IN GOD'S STRENGTH 75
CONCLUSION..84
HERE'S ANOTHER BOOK BY MARI SILVA THAT YOU MIGHT
LIKE 87
YOUR FREE GIFT (ONLY AVAILABLE FOR A LIMITED TIME) 88
REFERENCES...89
IMAGE SOURCES 93

Introduction

Spiritual warfare is not far-fetched or reserved for theologians or church leaders.

Whether you recognize it or not, it's a present, personal, and often silent battle you face daily. Warfare is real, and so is your victory in Christ. Spiritual Warfare Prayers is a complement to the book "Spiritual Warfare." It's your hands-on, Bible-centered companion guiding you daily through unseen battles. Unlike other warfare books that center on theories and abstract ideas, this book is practical, providing powerful prayers, scripture-based affirmations, and strategic study tools to help you engage and overcome spiritual battles.

This isn't merely another devotional or inspirational book. It's a battle manual for your daily spiritual needs. Each section is organized to provide quick and easy access to key guides to find exactly what you need. The book sheds light on unique daily struggles, like fighting fear, praying for strength in dark times, breaking generational strongholds, deliverance and protection, and seeking clarity in spiritual confusion. These are scripted to help you stand firm, pray boldly, and walk in victory. There are no fear-driven narratives, no vague mysticism, only plain, practical, and powerful Biblically grounded prayers to activate God's promises over your life.

Inside this book's pages are verses to strengthen your spirit, quotes to encourage your heart, and prayers to realign your mind with Christ's authority. If you've been seeking a book as a tool rather than mere encouragement, you've picked the right one. This book is full of God's word, and with the Word of God nigh to you and His victory in your heart, you can overcome whatever comes before you.

Chapter 1: The Bible Study of Spiritual Warfare

"For our struggle is not against flesh and blood, but against the rulers, against the authorities, against the powers of this dark world, and against the spiritual forces of evil in the heavenly realms." - Ephesians 6:12 NIV

Most believers have heard the term "Spiritual Warfare." However, many have no idea what it's about or how to identify one. This Chapter equips you with a solid Biblical understanding of spiritual warfare and ways to study and apply key principles for tackling it.

You need to understand the concept of spiritual warfare to overcome it.[1]

So, what is Spiritual Warfare?

Spiritual warfare is the conflict between the kingdom of God and the kingdom of darkness (Colossians 1:13). It's the action taken against Satan as he tries to keep you from accomplishing the call of God upon your life. The enemy desires to kill, steal, and destroy (John 10:10), and he would do everything within his power to carry out these actions as long as you are affiliated with Christ.

Spiritual warfare is real, and it's an ongoing battle between the kingdom of God and the forces of darkness, with many individuals being affected by it daily. These scars could be physical, emotional, psychological, and spiritual. For instance, in Matthew 4:1-11, when Jesus resisted the enemy in the wilderness, Eve was led astray (Genesis 3:1-7), or in Daniel 10:12-14, Daniel's prayer was being delayed by spiritual opposition.

Regardless of how the enemy initiates his attacks, directly or indirectly, encountering spiritual warfare is not a walk in the park. It tests your resolve, but approaching it properly will draw you closer to God.

Why Does Spiritual Warfare Occur, and How Does It Fit into God's Divine Plan?

Every believer in Christ will encounter spiritual warfare in one way or another. Also, not being in Christ doesn't exempt you from it, either. In His farewell speech, Jesus gave the following warning to His disciples, which is as useful then as it is now:

"I have said these things to you, that in me you may have peace. In the world you will have tribulation. But take heart; I have overcome the world." - John 16:33.

Job buttresses this further by stating, *"Man who is born of a woman is few of days and full of trouble* (Job 14:1).

Spiritual warfare occurs because:

You're in the World

Some schools of thought believe that those who do not follow God are punished with spiritual attacks. However, it is not entirely correct. Judging from the scriptural verses above, followers of God can face spiritual attacks. As long as you're in this sinful and decaying world, you're a target for the kingdom of darkness, which wants to stop you at all costs from coming into the light or remaining in it. The difference between the believer and the unbeliever is that the unbeliever doesn't stand a chance of facing these battles and coming out victorious like the believer. They continue to remain victims of the devil's attacks. However, it's sad that some believers live like victims because they do not know anything about spiritual welfare.

On the Road of Destiny

You might have heard this line before: "*You're going through tough times is proof that God is calling you into something greater, and the enemy wants to stop it.*" As cliché as that sounds, it's true. A stuck-up life going nowhere doesn't bother the enemy like one taking significant steps to fulfill God's calling. The enemy wouldn't sit a chance out. He will throw all he has in your direction to derail you from your destiny. Don't be discouraged. In time, things will turn out fine as long as you don't lose heart. Keep your faith and stand in God.

God uses spiritual warfare to shape you into His image, strengthen your faith, and grow and draw you to Himself (James 1:2-4). Therefore, stay strong, and do not lose heart because God is with you despite the struggles. "*Be strong and courageous. Do not be frightened, and do not be dismayed, for the LORD your God is with you wherever you go.*" - Deuteronomy 31:6 ESV

Satan's Methods/Strategies

"*Be sober-minded; be watchful. Your adversary, the devil, prowls around like a roaring lion, seeking someone to devour*" - 1 Peter 5:8

In this warfare, your adversary, the devil, is cunning and full of tricks. This is why the Apostles, Peter and Paul, admonished believers to always stay on guard and be on the lookout for Satan's schemes.

Methods and strategies used by the devil are:
Deception and Lies

"*And no wonder, for even Satan disguises himself as an angel of light.*" - 2 Corinthians 11:14 ESV

"*You are of your father the devil, and your will is to do your father's desires. He was a*

A statue of Satan.'

murderer from the beginning and does not stand in the truth, because there is no truth in him. When he lies, he speaks out of his character, for he is a liar and the father of lies." -John 8:44

Deception and lies are ways the enemy traps the believer to steal, kill, and destroy. The devil hates you because he hates God. This enmity is seen in his schemes to destroy you. How does he do that? He takes your focus and attention off God and channels it to the world or yourself through his oldest tool of deception and lies. He leads you astray when you least expect it, so you must remain watchful.

Do you remember how he came to Eve in Genesis 3:1-8? The Bible describes him as a cunning fellow who got to Eve through questions laced with deceit and lies. He succeeded in getting Eve's attention off God to herself when she desired to be like God. She questioned God's intentions and plans for her, which led to the fall of man. Satan knew if he could get Eve thinking "God was holding back on her" by twisting His word, he would turn her from God's path.

The devil is not new to this game, and while you may have lived a while on this Earth, he has lived for generations upon generations and has seen the rise and fall of kingdoms to refine, test-run, and perfect his schemes. He knows the weakness of men too well, and even Adam and Eve were no exception.

Temptation

"But each person is tempted when he is lured and enticed by his own desire. Then desire, when it has conceived, gives birth to sin, and sin, when it is fully grown, brings forth death." - James 1:14-15 ESV

This is another strategy of the enemy to entice and lure you away from God into destruction. He uses this tool more than others due to its effectiveness. Satan can't force or control you, so through your eye or ear gate, he brings thoughts and suggestions into your mind, causing you to sin. Satan's temptation could come as a direct or indirect attack. Direct temptation is the enemy tempting without a disguise. He often uses these methods on individuals who are trying hard to resist. For example, whether to cheat in an exam or getting bribed into doing something you know you shouldn't.

Indirect temptation comes through people, places, or things and is used more often because these mediums surround you. Satan doesn't need to do much before getting you to sin. He appeals to your senses - for instance, a catalog with beautiful women in the Magazine stand, or one delivered to your mailbox is enough to stir up lust and lead you to err. Another is anger or rage when someone cuts you off in traffic or bumps into you in a crowded walkway. Temptations will always appeal to your fleshly desires, and because your flesh loves feeling good, its desires are constantly fed by the enemy.

Fear

"There is no fear in love; but perfect love casts out fear because fear involves torment. But he who fears has not been made perfect in love." - 1 John 4:18 NKJV

Fear is a major strategy of the enemy against your faith – it kills faith. It's believing that something or someone is a threat to you. When you give in to fear, you remove your trust in God, expecting evil, pain, or danger. Fear is destructive; it kills dreams and hope, cripples, torments, and controls you. *It's no wonder the enemy enjoys using it.*

"For God gave us a spirit not of fear but of power and love and self-control." - 2 Timothy 1:7

When you don't feel power, love, and self-control, it is not coming from God. The main reason the enemy comes at you with a strategy of fear is because he wants to:

- Control and keep you bound
- Stop or ensure your spiritual growth is at a slower pace
- Reduce your faith in God
- Ensure you miss your calling
- Get you away from God, which is his main objective

Doubt

The enemy has used this strategy since the Garden of Eden when he came to Eve in Genesis 3:1-4 ESV. Eve fell for his schemes when she thought about the enemy's question. It is how the enemy sowed the seed of doubt in Eve and let her self-destruct:

"Now the serpent was more crafty than any other beast of the field that the Lord God had made. He said to the woman, "Did God actually say, 'You[a] shall not eat of any tree in the garden'?" And the woman said to the serpent, "We may eat of the fruit of the trees in the garden, but God said, 'You shall not eat of the fruit of the tree that is in the midst of the garden, neither shall you touch it, lest you die.'" But the serpent said to the woman, "You will not surely die."

Doubt is one way the devil moves you away from the Lord."

Satan uses this strategy to get you to shift ground by moving you away from God's ordained path. He can only kill or destroy you if he can get you away from your Safety (God). Satan wants you to doubt God's word (through questioning), like Zachariah questioning the Angel Gabriel (Luke 1:11-20). He wants you to doubt your salvation and God's mercy, grace, and love towards you. The end product of doubt is that you don't get anything from God.

"But let him ask in faith, with no doubting, for the one who doubts is like a wave of the sea that is driven and tossed by the wind. For that person must not suppose that he will receive anything from the Lord." - James 1:6-7

Key Biblical Principles of Overcoming Spiritual Attacks

The enemy is real, and so is the ongoing battle. The only way to come out on top is to know how to fight back and win.

Some biblical principles for overcoming Satan's attacks are:

Faith in Christ

"For everyone who has been born of God overcomes the world. And this is the victory that has overcome the world—our faith." - 1 John 5:4 ESV

Faith is a shield against Satan's fiery darts. It protects and helps deflect the enemy's attacks. What does it mean to have faith in Christ?

Hebrews 11:1 rightly answered: *"Now faith is confidence in what we hope for and assurance about what we do not see."*

Faith in Christ is beyond feelings; it's a conviction that God created the world, and Christ came to die for the sins of men so that they can have eternal life. This goes beyond knowledge to influence how you live. Like a shield protects the soldier in a battle, your faith can guard you in your trials. It protects you against Satan's scheme of doubt that causes you to question God's word and His Love for you. It's a shield against fear and anxiety and helps you to stand firm in your belief even during trials and challenges.

The power of the Word

"For the word of God is living and active, sharper than any two-edged sword, piercing to the division of soul and of spirit, of joints and of marrow, and discerning the thoughts and intentions of the heart." - Hebrews 4:12 ESV

The word of God is the sword of the Spirit.'

The word of God is the sword of the Spirit (Ephesians 6:17); it's alive and powerful. Spending time studying and committing scriptures to mind is one way to arm yourself with the truth of God's word, helping you combat the enemy's attacks. Jesus Christ demonstrated how to use the word when the enemy tempted Him in the wilderness. For the word to produce results, you must learn to give it voice by speaking it before the enemy attacks you.

"Every word of God proves true. He is a shield to all who come to him for protection."-Proverbs 30:5 NLT

Prayer and Fasting

"However, this kind does not go out except by prayer and fasting." - Matthew 17:21 NKJV

Prayer grants you direct access to God. It's when you come as a child before your Father to speak and hear from Him, express your concerns and desires, and seek His guidance. Fasting sets your heart on God; your flesh and desires are being crucified, so your spirit becomes sensitive to God and His leading.

God is sovereign and will forever be God. Engaging in a fast is not a hunger strike, nor is it an avenue to move God or bend His hands to come through for you. The aim is to cause your heart to align with God's will and ways. The strategy of prayer and fasting will cause Satanic influences or attacks to bow as the presence of God shines through you.

Authority in Christ

"Behold, I have given you authority to tread on serpents and scorpions, and over all the power of the enemy, and nothing shall hurt you." - Luke 10:19 ESV

"Submit yourselves, then, to God. Resist the devil, and he will flee from you." - James 4:7 NIV

This era is one of the fiercest times in human history, Biblically referred to as "the last days." Before Christ ascended, He gave you the authority to deal with these last days. However, to walk effectively in the authority of Christ, you must know:

What Authority Is

The authority you have in Christ means heaven's backing whenever you use and put your Faith in the Name of Jesus. It's similar to how a policeman pulls you over, not because he has the strength or power to do so by himself, but because he does it with the authority the State or country has bestowed on him. The same is true of the believer. You can step in front of an attack or difficulty, holding your hand out and saying, "Stop in the Name of Jesus!" because the Bible says everything responds to that name, and you were granted the right to use His name at any time.

That It Belongs to You

You have this authority because Jesus gave it to you (Luke 10:19). He received it from God the Father (Matthew 28:18). Christ is the head, and you're His body (Colossians 1:18). Since He is seated at the right hand of the Father in the heavenly places, you are also seated in the place of power and dominion (spiritual authority)- because where the head is, there the body is also. Christ gave you this spiritual authority to rule and reign in this life, so it's within your spiritual right to speak to the forces of darkness and tell them to be gone (Mark 16:15-18, Colossians 1:13)

How to Use It

You have to believe what God says about you in His word. Ponder over these scriptures (Ephesians 1:20 and Ephesians 2:6) till the light dawns on you. It's the key to exercising your authority in Christ. Only when you see yourself as Christ sees you, as His child who has His DNA and can do what He does, can you walk in the authority of Christ.

"Submit to God. Resist the devil and he will flee from you." - James 4:7. You have authority in Christ to overcome the enemy's attacks. God is in you and moves through you to ensure His will is done on Earth.

How to Study the Bible on Spiritual Warfare

Reading the Bible in a structured way will help you gain more substance from it.[5]

There is much to learn from the Bible. Here is a brief guide to help you get the most out of studying the word:

Read with Context

Reading the Bible in context (the entire passage) is vital to avoid misinterpretation instead of studying a few verses here and there.

Here is how to read with context:

- **Read the whole paragraph:** Read the paragraph surrounding your main verses. Usually, it shines the light needed to understand your main verse. For example, Philippians 4:13 says, *"I can do all things through him who strengthens me."* This sounds like a catchphrase to inspire you to accomplish things. However, looking at it contextually from verses 10 to 13 reveals how God infuses strength in you when you set your heart on contentment despite the difficulty.
- **Go through the whole book,** as it provides the context for the verse.
- **Learn the context within the Bible:** Every book, from Genesis to Revelation, tells a story of a loving God, which is interwoven in each chapter down to the verses. Knowing this helps you better appreciate studying the entire book. You don't have to do it in a rush. Enjoy each book, or get a good Bible reading plan and follow through with it.
- **Consider the Bible's plot:** Every scriptural passage fits into the following plot - the Creation (where mankind came from?), the Fall (How mankind failed), Redemption (God's solution to mankind's problems), and a New Creation (the future). As you study each passage, look for how these questions are answered.
- **Note the passages** that reveal more about who God is, His nature, and character.

Compare Scripture with Scripture

Only the Bible can answer the Bible's question, and no scripture is a private interpretation. When you study the Bible, you'll stumble on many instances when a verse from one book clarifies another in a different book. For example, a verse in Deuteronomy sheds light on a verse in Matthew, or a verse in Daniel gives meaning to one in Revelation. This is also true of spiritual warfare themes throughout the Old and New Testaments.

For instance:

"Finally, be strong in the Lord and in the strength of his might. Put on the whole armor of God, that you may be able to stand against the schemes of the devil. For we do not wrestle against flesh and blood, but against the rulers, against the authorities, against the cosmic powers over

this present darkness, against the spiritual forces of evil in the heavenly places. Therefore, take up the whole armor of God, that you may be able to withstand in the evil day, and having done all, to stand firm. Stand therefore, having fastened on the belt of truth, and having put on the breastplate of righteousness, and, as shoes for your feet, having put on the readiness given by the gospel of peace. In all circumstances, take up the shield of faith, with which you can extinguish all the flaming darts of the evil one; and take the helmet of salvation, and the sword of the Spirit, which is the word of God, praying at all times in the Spirit, with all prayer and supplication. To that end, keep alert with all perseverance, making supplication for all the saints." - Ephesians 6:10-18

"For though we walk in the flesh, we are not waging war according to the flesh. For the weapons of our warfare are not of the flesh but have divine power to destroy strongholds. We destroy arguments and every lofty opinion raised against the knowledge of God, and take every thought captive to obey Christ." - 2 Corinthians 10:3-5

Meditate and Memorize Key Verses

Memorization enhances meditation. When you spend time on a passage and are not in a hurry to jump to the next one but savor every verse or line of a verse, it stays with you. It's how you become shaped by the scriptures. Writing in journals and committing to scripture memorization helps in meditation. As effort is put into memorizing scriptures, more time is spent on the word, which solidifies in your heart.

Do you want to memorize and meditate on key verses? Start with the following spiritual warfare verses:

- *"Submit yourselves therefore to God. Resist the devil, and he will flee from you."* - James 4:7
- *"Be sober-minded; be watchful. Your adversary, the devil, prowls around like a roaring lion, seeking someone to devour."* - 1 Peter 5:8
- *"Behold, I have given you authority to tread on serpents and scorpions, and over all the power of the enemy, and nothing shall hurt you."* - Luke 10:19
- *"The Lord will cause your enemies who rise against you to be defeated before you. They shall come out against you one way and flee before you seven ways."* - Deuteronomy 28:7

- *"No weapon that is fashioned against you shall succeed, and you shall refute every tongue that rises against you in judgment. This is the heritage of the servants of the Lord and their vindication from me, declares the Lord." - Isaiah 54:17*

Use Study Tools

Study tools help determine translational variations between passages and the meaning of a passage and guide you in studying within a historical context. With study tools, you can easily apply the lessons learned from the Bible to your life. Below are study tools to enhance deeper understanding:

- **Concordance:** Everyday Access, Your Bible Concordance, The New Thematic Concordance, Strong's Guide to Bible Words.
- **Commentaries:** High-Definition Commentary Collection, Tyndale Commentaries, Lexham Context Commentary: New Testament.
- **Word Studies:** ESV study Bible, CBS study Bible, Vine's Complete Expository Dictionary of Old and New Testament words.

Apply the Word in Prayer

Let the word of God be the basis of your prayer life. As you study the word and it speaks to you, especially on spiritual warfare, you can turn it into prayer by saying the exact word or rewording it as the Holy Spirit leads you.

Here is how:

- Start by restating God's truth while affirming your faith. For instance, *"Father, thank you for you are good and your mercy endureth forever."* - 1 Chronicles 16:34
- Tell Him about the passages you want reflected in your life. For instance, Father, you said in your Word that *"whoever says he abides in him ought to walk in the same way in which he walked."* - 1 John 2:6. Please help me understand and walk like Christ so I can live up to the standard Christ expects of me.
- Then, ask for specific needs like protection and strength. For example, *"Lord, you are my refuge, and I put my trust in you, and so I am not forsaken."* - Psalms 9: 9-10

- Praise God in your paraphrased words of scripture: *"Lord, I thank you because I know that you're with me despite the challenges before me. I praise you because you will never leave nor forsake me."* - Hebrews 13:5

This shows you how to pray God's Word.

Having established a Biblical understanding of spiritual warfare and how to study and apply key principles for tackling it in this chapter, the following chapters provide specific prayers and scripture-based strategies for various aspects of spiritual warfare.

Chapter 2: The Armor of God: Verses to Equip Yourself for Battle

"Finally, my brethren, be strong in the Lord and in the power of His might... Put on the whole armor of God, that you may be able to stand against the wiles of the devil...." - Ephesians 6:10-11 NKJV

Apostle Paul emphasizes that believers should always be on guard in this scripture. The urgency of this command is seen in verse 11: *"Put on the whole armor of God, that you may be able to stand against the wiles of the devil."* The Bible makes it clear that the devil won't relent; he is constantly waging attacks against you, and God has freely given you this armor of spiritual defense against him. You are expected to actively put on the full armor of God to stay alert and withstand the enemy in spiritual warfare.

"Be sober, be vigilant; because your adversary the devil walks about like a roaring lion, seeking whom he may devour." - 1 Peter 5:8 NKJV

The armor of God is divinely given because you can't fight the enemy with your human strength or power. Explore the armor of God and what each piece represents in this chapter.

The Belt of Truth

"Stand firm then, with the belt of truth buckled around your waist." - Ephesians 6:14a NIV

In ancient times – and even now – the belt buckled around the Roman soldiers' waists were known to hold every other piece of the armor in place. This shows its importance. As a believer, this belt signifies the truth of God's Word that holds your faith firmly, so you stand strong, believing God's promises over your and your family's lives. Living in this truth makes you immune to the devil's lies and tricks. Your life is free from his antics of deception and spiritual confusion because you are firmly rooted in the truth and Jesus.

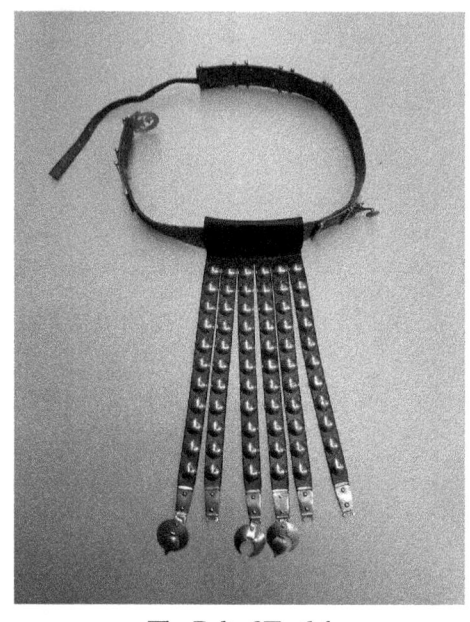

The Belt of Truth.⁶

"Then you will know the truth, and the truth will set you free." - John 8:32 NIV

"Sanctify them by Your truth. Your word is truth." - John 17:17 NKJV

For instance, as a student, the devil may deceive you into thinking that you aren't capable of passing your exams. When you find this darkness lurking, you should immediately declare God's truth in Philippians 4:13, *"I can do all things through Christ who strengthens me."* The truth of God's Word is an armor that constantly keeps your faith firm in God and the finished work of His son, Jesus Christ, and renders the enemy powerless over you.

Daily Prayer

As you continuously decree and believe God's Word over your life, say this prayer daily: *"Father, I pray that You grant me the power to walk in the truth of Your Word, and to discern the devil's lies and tricks. I pray against deception that leads me away from Your plan and purpose for me, in Jesus' name, Amen."*

The Breastplate of Righteousness

"...with righteousness as your breastplate." - Ephesians 6:14b GNT

The Roman soldiers used well-crafted breastplates as a defense to protect vital organs, like their hearts and lungs, during battle. As a child of God and an active soldier of the Lord's Army, you can use the breastplate of righteousness as a spiritual defense to guard your heart in spiritual warfare against your adversary, the devil. Many instances in the Bible show the heart as essential for a believer.

The Breastplate of Righteousness.'

"For it is by believing in his heart that a man becomes right with God." - Romans 10:10 TLB

"Guard your heart above all else, for it determines the course of your life." - Proverbs 4:23 NLT

You have been called and empowered to live a life of righteousness in Christ Jesus (through His finished work on the cross). Living righteously means you are to guard your heart to avoid sin and rely wholly on the righteousness of Christ Jesus.

"Christ was without sin, but for our sake God made him share our sin in order that in union with him we might share the righteousness of God." - 2 Corinthians 5:21 GNT

"Righteousness [moral and spiritual integrity and virtuous character] exalts a nation, but sin is a disgrace to any people." - Proverbs 14:34 AMP

When you put on this armor of righteousness in Christ as a spiritual defense, the enemy's attacks can't get to you.

Daily Prayer

Say this prayer daily: *"Lord, I pray You create in me a pure and new heart, I decree against every chain of shame and guilt. I pray for the strength to resist temptations from the enemy, and hold on to Your finished work for me. Help me see that I'm made righteous in Your righteousness, not by my work. In Jesus' name, Amen."*

The Shoes of the Gospel of Peace

"...and having shod your feet with the preparation of the gospel of peace." - Ephesians 6:15 NKJV

During battles, ease of movement is essential to a soldier. Soldiers with inadequate footwear would find it difficult to move freely, tactically, and engage properly in battle. The early Roman soldiers wore solid footwear that gave them stability in battles. Your footwear as a believer in spiritual warfare is the Gospel of Peace, which gives you maximum stability to walk firm in the faith. You can share this Gospel of Christ without fear and stand firmly in its spiritual peace.

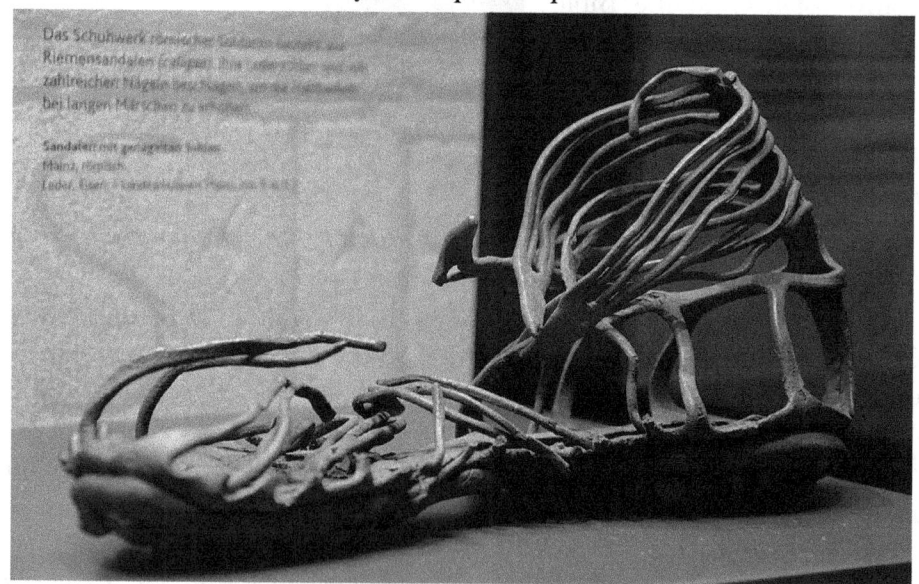

The Shoes of the Gospel of Peace.⁸

"How beautiful upon the mountains are the feet of him who brings good news, who proclaims peace, who brings glad tidings of good things, who proclaims salvation, who says to Zion, 'Your God reigns!'" - Isaiah 52:7 NKJV

"And He said to them, "Go into all the world and preach the gospel to all creation."" - Mark 16:15 AMP

Daily Prayer

Say this prayer daily to help you share this Gospel of Peace around your world: *"Father, I pray for grace and confidence to share the Gospel of Peace among people You've placed around me. Let my daily presence and dealings shine a light on Your glorious gospel. In Jesus' name, Amen."*

The Shield of Faith

"Above all, lift up the [protective] shield of faith with which you can extinguish all the flaming arrows of the evil one." - Ephesians 6:16 AMP

The Bible describes faith as a protective shield against the enemy's attack, like a Roman soldier uses a strong protective shield to defend himself against the enemy's flaming arrows in battle.

"Now faith is the substance of things hoped for, the evidence of things not seen." - Hebrews. 11:1 NKJV

Faith, as a part of the armor of God, is a shield to protect you from the devil's lies and his attacks, like fears and doubts. In challenging situations, your firm faith (belief) in God and His Word casts away fears.

The Shield of Faith.⁹

"For God has not given us a spirit of fear, but of power and of love and of a sound mind." - 2 Timothy 1:7 NKJV

As a believer in spiritual warfare, one way to defeat the enemy is to actively trust every Word of God, stand strong on His promises, and remove doubt from your mind entirely.

"Now faith is the assurance (title deed, confirmation) *of things hoped for* (divinely guaranteed)*, and the evidence of things not seen* [the conviction of their reality - faith comprehends what cannot be experienced by the physical senses]."* - Hebrews 11:1 AMP

"But he must ask [for wisdom] *in faith, without doubting* [God's willingness to help]*, for the one who doubts is like a billowing surge of the sea that is blown about and tossed by the wind."* - James 1:6 AMP

Daily Prayer

Say this simple prayer of faith throughout your day: *"Father, I thank You for Your great promises over my life. I ask for unwavering faith to believe and hold on to Your promises even when it seems impossible. I cast out every spirit of fear and doubt and pray for the strength to resist the enemy's lie. In Jesus' name, Amen.*

The Helmet of Salvation

"...and take the helmet of salvation." - Ephesians 6:17a NKJV

The head controls the mind, actions, and behavior of the body. Therefore, it must be well-protected by a strong helmet when in battle. You, the believer in spiritual warfare, have been given the free gift of salvation (through the finished work of Christ) as a helmet to protect your head and mind from the enemy's attack. It connotes constantly renewing your mind in Christ, laying hold of your salvation and awakening to righteousness, rejecting anything that brings you fear, ignoring the devil's condemnations, who the Bible describes as "the accuser of the brethren," and staying in your conviction of Jesus Christ and your identity in Him.

The Helmet of Salvation.[10]

"...and do not be conformed to this world, but be transformed by the renewing of your mind, that you may prove what is that good and acceptable and perfect will of God." - Romans 12:2 NKJV

"Casting down arguments and every high thing that exalts itself against the knowledge of God, bringing every thought into captivity to the obedience of Christ." - 2 Corinthians 10:5 NKJV

Daily Prayer

Say this daily prayer to put on the helmet of salvation against the enemy's attack: *"Lord, I ask You to grant me mental and spiritual clarity in all I do, protect my mind from the deceptions of the enemy and give me the grace always to remember and keep walking in this great gift of salvation You have given me, in Jesus' name, Amen."*

The Sword of The Spirit

"...and the sword of the Spirit, which is the Word of God." - Ephesians 6:17b

The sword of the Spirit in God's armor is the only offensive weapon of spiritual defense. God's Word is so powerful that it defeats the enemy immediately when you use it in spiritual warfare. While praying, you can boldly speak and declare God's Word in the scriptures over what you are praying about. It shows your faith in His Word and reminds the enemy of his defeat. Use God's Word to resist the temptations the enemy throws at you – as Jesus did in Matthew 4:1-11

"Then Jesus was led up by the Spirit into the wilderness to be tempted by the devil. And when He had fasted forty days and forty nights, afterward He was hungry. Now when the tempter came to Him, he said, "If You are the Son of God, command that these stones become bread." But He answered and said, "It is written, 'Man shall not live by bread alone, but by every word that proceeds from the mouth of God.' Then the devil took Him up into the holy city, set Him on the pinnacle of the temple and said to Him, "If You are the Son of God, throw Yourself down. For it is written: "He shall give His angels charge over you, and in their hands they shall bear you up, lest you dash your foot against a stone.

Jesus said to him, "It is written again, 'You shall not tempt the Lord your God.'" Again, the devil took Him up on an exceedingly high mountain, and showed Him all the kingdoms of the world and their glory. And he said to Him, "All these things I will give You if You will

fall down and worship me." Then Jesus said to him, *"Away with you, Satan! For it is written, 'You shall worship the Lord your God, and Him only you shall serve."* Then the devil left Him, and behold, angels came and ministered to Him."* - Matthew 4:1-11 NKJV

You can see how Jesus used the Word of God to defeat the enemy and his attacks. You can do the same. When praying or in a tough situation, boldly declaring God's Word over the situation with faith, you can expect to come out strong and victorious.

Daily Prayer

Say this prayer daily: *"Lord, I pray for the wisdom to use the right scriptures to declare Your Word over my situation authoritatively. I pray that You grant me strength and victory in my spiritual battles, in Jesus' name, Amen."*

The Power of Prayer

"Praying always with all prayer and supplication in the Spirit, being watchful to this end with all perseverance and supplication for all the saints." - Ephesians 6:18 NKJV

After Apostle Paul had listed the armor of God that you are expected to put on as a believer, he ended by giving a crucial command: He asked every believer to pray continually. As a believer, you must know that prayer is a powerful tool in spiritual warfare. The armor is ineffective without prayer, so commit to praying always.

"The prayer of a righteous person is powerful and effective." - James 5:16b NIV

"Pray continually" - 1 Thessalonians 5:17 NIV

During life battles, always stay alert and seek God through prayer. Don't get tired of praying because it's a strong spiritual tool. When you combine prayers and the armor of God, you can successfully defeat the enemy in spiritual warfare. So, develop a habit of praying often and relying on the help and power of the Holy Spirit.

Daily Prayer

Say this prayer daily: *"Lord, give me the grace and strength to pray always, even when I may not feel like praying, help me stay committed and dedicated to You. Father, equip my spirit to stay alert and always rely on Your Holy Spirit. In Jesus' name, Amen."*

Now, as a believer knowing about the armor of God and what it means to gain victory in spiritual warfare, pray through each piece of the armor in your daily prayers. Continually ask God for His protection and strength to help you use each armor fully.

For example:

"Heavenly Father, I come before You today, recognizing the spiritual battles around me. Help me to be strong in Your power and to stand firm against the enemy. I now put on the full armor of God: I fasten the belt of truth around my waist. Guide me to live in honesty and integrity, holding firmly to Your Word as my foundation. I wear the breastplate of righteousness. Protect my heart from sin and guilt. Help me to walk in obedience, trusting in Christ's righteousness. I fit my feet with the shoes of peace, ready to stand firm and share the gospel wherever You lead me. Let Your peace calm my heart and guide my steps. I take up the shield of faith. Strengthen my trust in You so that I can extinguish every fiery arrow of doubt, fear, and temptation. I put on the helmet of salvation. Guard my mind with the knowledge of my salvation. Remind me of the hope and victory I have in Christ. I take the sword of the Spirit, which is Your Word. Teach me to use Scripture as a weapon to combat the enemy's lies and to speak the truth in every situation. Finally, Lord, I pray in the Spirit on all occasions. Keep me alert and prayerful for myself and others. Thank You for equipping me for this battle. In Jesus' name, Amen."

Chapter 3: Prayers for Strength in Times of Darkness

God never allows His child to be in the dark without providing an escape. The scriptures regard Him as all-knowing (Omniscient), all-powerful (Omnipotent), and an ever-present help in times of need (Omnipresent). In a fallen world such as this, there are times when darkness is all around, surging, trying to overpower and overshadow you. In these times, you need more than human strength to overcome.

Prayers will get you through times of darkness.[11]

God has made prayer a point of access to Him. It's how you draw strength from God's divine source and tap into His divine wisdom and powers to counter every darkness around you. The scriptures say in Genesis 1 that in the beginning, there was utter darkness (signifying the issues of life), and the Earth was without form and void (signifying chaos and confusion). What God did when He saw these was not to lose hope but to call forth light amid this darkness. The power to triumph in a situation and for strength in dark times is available in prayers.

Prayer is a lifeline connecting you with God's presence when you feel weak, discouraged, and attacked. The presence of God brings much into a person's life:

"The Lord is my strength and song, And He has become my salvation; He is my God, and I will praise Him; My Father's God, and I will exalt Him. The Lord is a man of war; The Lord is His name. Your right hand, O Lord, has become glorious in power; Your right hand, O Lord, has dashed the enemy in pieces." - Exodus 15:2-3, 6

God understands it's inevitable to lose strength and feel weary and discouraged in this world. Even Jesus lost strength when He looked at the battles before Him. However, Jesus didn't dwell in this downtrodden state but prayed to God. The Bible described how He prayed so fervently that His sweat became thick and dropped like blood to the ground. If Jesus could lose strength, as with the other prophets and significant people in the Bible, then know this is inevitable. Sometimes, it looks like the darkness is too overpowering, but cheer up; there is hope. The darkness could not overshadow the light of God, and you are God's light in this dark world.

Spiritual Darkness and How to Overcome It

When you overcome spiritual darkness, you move into a greater glory. However, when you experience it, you can't comprehend it. Spiritual darkness appears as doubt, fear, discouragement, weariness, and weakness, which draw you away from God, not because God distances Himself from you, but because it creates an illusion that you're far from His presence and help.

Life's stressors happen to every person. However, for Christians, they should be seen and handled spiritually. The enemies take no joy in seeing you prosper and dominate and will do anything to see you fail.

However, God has provided you with His armor (this was extensively discussed in the first book). You understand by now that your enemy, the devil, is resilient. He knows how protected you are by God but will throw shade at you to test your faith and confidence in God.

The place of spiritual attacks is what leads to spiritual darkness, and you can get spiritually attacked in many ways. For example, attacks can be the loss of a dearly loved one, criticism, bullying, job loss, financial battles, temptations to compromise your faith, isolation, uncertainties, and many other battles. As easy as these may have been written, they are not easy to bear. These battles can break you, weigh you down, make you doubt your stance in God, or isolate you from God and people. However, the Bible shares the Good News that even amid darkness, you're not alone:

"The righteous cry out, and the Lord hears, and delivers them out of all their troubles. The Lord is near to those who have a broken heart, And saves such as have a contrite spirit." - Psalms 34:17-18

Prayer is like tapping a partner in a ring fight to enter the ring. When you pray, you invite the presence of God to deliver you from your troubles. The devil's attack creates a darkness that burdens you, making you feel too weak or discouraged to ask God for help. Throughout the Bible are stories of people who fought through darkness and overcame. A careful study of these men and women reveals how they handled the matters that befell them.

Here are a few of these Bible characters:

David

David's struggles and battles were almost too obvious for anyone to deny. He was a target to men and the devil from the day he was anointed by God's prophet.

Reading the book of Samuel, you may only see a fraction of his external battles, but when you study deeper, especially studying the book of Psalms, you will realize he also had many internal battles.

He was despised, betrayed, and persecuted by those he loved and trusted; he was lied to, plotted against, insulted, and chased around like an outcast. David faced these and more, and you will realize his deep struggles when you read the book of Psalms.

However, the book of Psalms is powerful because it shows how David's tears and Joy were directed to God in prayers. He documented and offered to God his struggles in exchange for God's presence and help. David's pain drove him to a timely, intimate, and ultimate dependence on the Lord. Every chapter in Psalms can be dangerous to call down the timely intervention of God. Whatever struggle or experience, there is a Psalm for you.

"*My God, My God, why have You forsaken Me? Why are You so far from helping me, And from the words of my groaning? O, My God, I cry in the daytime, but You do not hear; And in the night season, and am not silent.*" - Psalms 22:1-2 NKJV

The above scripture shows David crying in anguish while contemporaneously trusting in the Most High.

"*God is our refuge and strength, A very present help in trouble.*" - Psalms 46:1

Elijah

"*But he himself went a day's journey into the wilderness, and came and sat down under a broom tree. And he prayed that he might not die, and said, "It is enough! Now, Lord, take my life, for I am no better than my fathers!" Then as he lay and slept under a broom tree, suddenly an angel touched him, and said to him, "Arise and eat." Then he looked, and there by his head was a cake baked on coals, and a jar of water. So, he ate and drank, and lay down again. And the angel of the Lord came back the second time, and touched him, and said, "Arise and eat, because the journey is too great for you." So, he arose, and ate and drank; and he went in the strength of that food forty days and forty nights as far as Horeb, the mountain of God.*" - 1 Kings 19:4-8

A painting of Prophet Elijah.[13]

Although a prophet of God, Elijah was a man like everyone else. He commanded fire from heaven yet ran into hiding when threatened by a woman. How can one command the power of God so greatly in one moment and completely flee at the rise of trouble? You must know this is entirely humanlike, and God understands. He didn't judge Elijah when he went into hiding from a person; he only called him unto Himself and strengthened him.

It is normal to fear when situations stir up, but you must rest on the assurance that God is with you and won't let the worries and chaos around you consume you. Trust God when you should naturally fear - trust and faith are the opposite of fear.

Jesus

He was the Son of God, yet He was in human flesh and felt all your burdens.

"Then Jesus came with them to a place called Gethsemane, and said to the disciples, "Sit here while I go and pray over there. "And He took with Him Peter and the two sons of Zebedee, and He began to be sorrowful and deeply distressed. Then He said to them, "My soul is exceedingly sorrowful, even to death. Stay here and watch with Me." He went a little farther and fell on His face, and prayed, saying, "O My Father, if it is possible, let this cup pass from Me; nevertheless, not as I will, but as You will." - Matthew 26:36-39

Jesus' first reaction to his burdens and issues was prayer. He must've carried the burden of His approaching death for so long that it weighed down His soul. In darkness, Jesus resorted to prayer for several hours, three times on the same night. After praying, He received strength from God to face the cross and death, and in the end, He rose into much glory. The Scripture says:

"Looking unto Jesus, the author and finisher of our faith, who for the joy that was set before Him endured the cross, despising the shame, and has sat down at the right hand of the throne of God. For consider Him who endured such hostility from sinners against Himself, lest you become weary and discouraged in your souls." - Hebrews 12:2-3

How much more can it be proven that it's good to trust in God? He made His Son and prophets live through these issues to set good examples for believers. Then He made His Son experience the burdened life of a human, so when He intercedes for you (Romans 8:34), it is from depth because He once lived as a man.

"For we do not have a High Priest who cannot sympathize with our weaknesses, but was in all points tempted as we are, yet without sin. Let us therefore come boldly to the throne of grace, that we may obtain mercy and find grace to help in time of need." - Hebrews 4:15-16

The Importance of Praying for Strength as a Christian

Prayer isn't only a request for relief. It's a way to connect with God. Endless possibilities are transferred to you in this connection. Your request may have been for strength, but through prayer, God can supply wisdom, resilience, power, a shift in perspective, patience, self-control, and endurance. God is always ready to connect with you and draw you closer to Him.

Sometimes, God permits darkness to come your way to increase your strength or prepare you for greater glory. For example, losing a job could make you unstable financially and cause immense concern, but God could have seen a danger ahead in your current position. Losing that job is God looking out for you. If you go through this phase of seeming darkness without trusting and asking Him for strength, you might be totally drained or too overwhelmed to enter the victory that follows.

Whenever you pray to God, He always sends His help of strength to lead you through the darkness and help you overcome challenges. Being open and ready for God's answers when you pray is crucial. When people pray, they sometimes zero in on the answers they want. If they don't find the issue ending at that moment, they become more burdened or lose trust in God. You connect to God when you pray and, in turn, receive strength and boldness to face the burden and win.

Learn to trust God and know He always has your best interests at heart. Prepare yourself for the answers and know that even when you may not initially agree with or like them, God sees ahead and knows better, so it's wise to lean on Him. What follows after the prayer for strength is peace. When you pray for strength, God strengthens your soul with peace through His Holy Spirit and Word. It's through the assurance from His Word that you feel His Peace.

Here's a practical recap - When the enemy attacks in discouragement, anxiety, doubt, fear, and depression, your first resort should be prayer. Pray for strength and with an open mind when you pray. Do not fear presenting your matter before God - if it's a doubt, tell Him. Let Him know your thoughts towards Him and the matter, and ask Him to help you with strength. Do not attempt to solve the matter if God hasn't spoken. God speaks in many ways: His Word, your Christian or close friends, mentors, teachers, or a quiet, small voice. When you are open, you position yourself better to get answers faster.

"But those who wait on the Lord Shall renew their strength; They shall mount up with wings like eagles, They shall run and not be weary, They shall walk and not faint." - Isaiah 40:31

The attacks mentioned are not the problems, like losing a job or getting involved in an accident. They are events, not the real attack; the enemy only uses them as a tool to pose an attack. The true attack is on your faith. So, how you handle these challenges matters significantly. When you wait on God in prayer, He will surely renew your strength, and your comeback will be much greater in dealing with the issues. As explained in Chapter One, searching for Bible verses that tally with your circumstances and praying for them helps.

Always give yourself this assurance:

"I can do all things through Christ who strengthens me." - Philippians 4:13

Four Methods of Praying for Strength

When you pray for strength, your answers come in various ways. Sometimes, strength can come from encouraging words or receiving help precisely when needed.

There are four main methods for praying.[18]

Four practical methods of praying for strength are:

1. Pray God's Promises:

In praying and declaring God's promises, you bank and trust in the assurance of His Word that if He did it before, He will do it again. God has said that he honors His Word more than His name. You are expected to do likewise, not by dishonoring His name but by proclaiming the truth of His Word. As you pray, search the scriptures for the promises pertaining to you, then pray with them, and genuinely believe that God hears your prayers.

"By which have been given to us exceedingly great and precious promises, that through these you may be partakers of the divine nature...." - *2* Peter 1:4

2. Be Specific:

As you pray, learn to itemize your struggles before God openly. Do not feel ashamed or scared to present the real issues before Him, no matter how odd or dark you think they are. If there is anyone who understands you better, it's your heavenly Father. The more open you are to God in prayer, the more places you provide for Him to help you.

"He shall call upon Me, and I will answer him; I will be with him in trouble; I will deliver him and honor him. With long life I will satisfy him, And show him my salvation." - Psalms 91:15-16

3. Surrender Burdens:

It's not enough to search for the promises and tell God about that issue. You must surrender and let Him handle it as He sees fit. Often, people pray and feel unsatisfied with the speed of the answer, then take matters into their own hands, which takes them outside the will of God. A part of trust is surrender - if you've prayed and laid something in God's hands, don't take it back. Jesus cares for you. Hence, He says to cast your burden on him. He will carry them for you.

"Casting all your care upon Him, for He cares for you." I Peter 5:7

4. Seek the Holy Spirit's Guidance:

After surrendering all to God, you can ask for discernment and a steadfast faith. As a believer, you have the gift of the Holy Spirit in you to lead you into all truth (John 16:13). When this happens, you can continue in faith and discern when the devil throws more shade to dim your light and rob your strength, and perceive God's directions.

"The Lord will guide you continually, and satisfy your soul in drought, and strengthen your bones; You shall be like a watered garden, and like a spring of water, whose waters do not fail." - Isaiah 58:11

Applying Practical Prayer Habits

Prayer is a lifestyle and one of your greatest tools as a child of God. When you study the scriptures carefully, you know that Jesus intercedes for the church in prayer. You will discover that the Spirit prays for you continually (Romans 8:26-27). Before prayer can become your lifestyle, it must become a habit, and habits are forged via discipline or love. For example, you can be in love with someone so much that you don't need a reminder to talk to them every day.

On the other hand, you may need someone so much (they serve a great purpose for your life's destination) that you must communicate with them through discipline. It is the same with prayer. You can develop a prayer habit out of necessity or love. The aim is to reach a great desire to always fellowship with God.

Practical habits to keep you praying are:

- **Keep a Prayer Journal:** A prayer journal helps you keep track of current results from past prayers. This journal lets you see and track God's faithfulness in your life. It enables you to practice gratitude and reduce worries, especially on days when you lose strength and events make you question God. Besides this, jot down things you want to talk to God about. Journaling helps you pour your heart out better.

- **Memorize Key Scriptures:** Keeping scriptures at heart is healthy, for instance, in a sudden attack when you need to seek peace from God's Word. You'll benefit greatly from your wealth of memorized scriptures. Also, it keeps you praying God's Word, even on the go.

    Strength-boosting scriptures to memorize are:

    "Yea, though I walk through the valley of the shadow of death, I will fear no evil; For You are with me; Your rod and Your staff, they comfort me." – Psalms 23:4

    "Fear not, for I am with you; Be not dismayed, for I am your God. I will strengthen you, Yes, I will help you, I will uphold you with My righteous right hand." - Isaiah 41:10

- **Set a Regular Prayer Time:** Start small, start daily, and build your prayer time consistently. Set a time daily to pray for strength for yourself and others. It doesn't have to be long hours; 5-10 minutes to start is good enough. Do not wait for the perfect time because there is no better time to begin than now.
- **Pray and Intercede for Others:** You can intercede alone or join a Christian group or community. There is much to intercede for; many people go through weakness and spiritual darkness but don't know how to overcome it. Let your prayer be a rescue.

"Again, I say to you that if two of you agree on earth concerning anything that they ask, it will be done for them by My Father in heaven. For where two or three are gathered together in My name, I am there in the midst of them." - Matthew 18:19-20

Prayers for Strength

Practical ways to pray for strength are:

Prayer for Strength in Overwhelming Times: *"Heavenly Father, I feel weak and burdened by the struggles around me, but I trust in Your promise that You are my refuge and strength, an ever-present help in trouble (Psalm 46:1). Fill me with Your Peace, courage, and hope. Renew my spirit, and help me stand firm in faith. In Jesus' name, Amen."*

Prayer for the Strength to Stand Firm: *"Father, I feel under attack, but I know You have given me victory through Jesus Christ. Strengthen me to stand firm and resist the enemy's lies with Your truth. I declare that no weapon formed against me shall prosper (Isaiah 54:17). Help me put on the full armor of God and stand strong in faith. In Jesus' name, Amen."*

Spiritual darkness spans from darts thrown by the enemies, and as a believer, these darts are thrown at you with or without your whole armor on. An effect of these attacks is a loss of strength in the soul. Even though Jesus lost strength, what He did afterward showed us how to handle these circumstances. Your first resort should be prayer - pray God's promise, pray specific prayers for strength, surrender your burden to Jesus, and allow the Holy Spirit to lead you. Know that you're never alone; God is with you even until the end of the age.

AREAS I NEED STRENGTH

Search your heart and write down areas you need God's strength:

_____
_____
_____
_____
_____
_____
_____
_____
_____

PRAYERS

Put these areas into prayer:

_____
_____
_____
_____
_____
_____
_____
_____
_____
_____
_____

Chapter 4: Bible Verses for Victory in Warfare

There was a popular TV show titled "Forged in Fire," where blacksmiths and masters of their crafts from various walks of life competed. With the materials and little time allotted, these blacksmiths were to forge weapons and blades. The judges would try the forged

Some prayers are useful when going into battle.[14]

blades against various objects. Among the judges was a US Air Force Veteran and a martial artist who had spent years training first responders and military personnel. He was in charge of testing the blades' sharpness and lethality by slicing and stabbing leather pillows, pig carcasses, etc. Any blades that survived the testing process received positive feedback, such as "It will K.E.AI" from this veteran. K.E.AI is an acronym for "Keep Everyone Alive." Hence, your weapon, beyond being able to wreak physical havoc on anyone or anything, should protect you and everyone around you.

How Bible Verses Help in Warfare

Satan doesn't mind you the way you are, but the moment you declare the Lordship of Jesus over your life, you sign yourself up for more spiritual warfare. This is why you have the armor to keep you safe from the weight of the enemy's attacks - whether depression, anxiety, or despair.

Learning Bible verses will help you in warfare as follows:

By Renewing Your Mind

"Do not be conformed to this world (this age), [fashioned after and adapted to its external, superficial customs], but be transformed (changed) by the [entire] renewal of your mind [by its new ideals and its new attitude], so that you may prove [for yourselves] what is the good and acceptable and perfect will of God, even the thing which is good and acceptable and perfect [in His sight for you]." - Romans 12:2 AMPC

The enemy doesn't fight fairly and will do everything in his power to stop you from being all God has called you to be. As you have learned in previous chapters, the enemy does this through weapons of deception and bombards your mind with negative thoughts. John 8:44 describes the enemy as a liar who aims to lure you into his web of lies. Therefore, the Word of God helps renew your mind. Meditating on scriptures transforms how you think and aligns your thoughts with the truth of God's Word, enabling you to discern anything contrary.

Furthermore, 2 Corinthians 10:4-5 NKJV says, *"The weapons of our warfare are not carnal but mighty in God for pulling down strongholds, casting down arguments and every high thing that exalts itself against the knowledge of God, bringing every thought into captivity to the obedience of Christ."*

Strongholds, a battle term, are areas in your mind where the enemy has invaded and taken control. They are where the devil has successfully won you over through deception. How does he do this? By flooding your mind with thoughts inconsistent with the Word of God. When these thoughts take root (a stronghold), they lead to doubt, fear, suspicion, conspiracy theories, and reasoning that don't align with the truth of God's Word. In renewing your mind, the Word of God is the most potent and powerful weapon that destroys every stronghold and changes you from the inside out as you learn, read, study, and live God's Word.

By Declaring Victory

"But thanks be to God, who gives us the victory [making us conquerors] through our Lord Jesus Christ." - 1 Corinthians 15:57 AMP

"Now thanks be to God who always leads us in triumph in Christ, and through us diffuses the fragrance of His knowledge in every place." - 2 Corinthians 2:14 NKJV

Positive affirmations are good, but they can only go so far. The last thing you want to declare is the world's wisdom (positive affirmations) and not God's wisdom (1 Corinthians 2:6-7) in spiritual influences and opposition. Your triumph (victory) over the enemy is tied to your cooperation with God's Word about your identity in Christ, *by speaking God's Word aloud.* When God speaks, things change; when you speak the Word, the situation has no choice but to respond to you because the word of God in your mouth is like the word in His mouth. Also, reading or speaking the word aloud resonates with peace. It reinforces and strengthens your faith as a reminder that you have the authority of Christ.

By declaring your victory, you speak faith, not fear, professing what you want to see, not what you are experiencing. Remember, Jesus defeated the enemy in the wilderness by declaring the scriptures aloud, "It is written" (Matthew 4:1-11). Declare only thoughts aligning with His Word, despite pressures or oppositions, and immediately refuse alternatives.

By Strengthening Faith

"So, then faith cometh by hearing, and hearing by the Word of God." - Romans 10:17 KJV

Faith is born in your heart when you dwell on the Word of God. As often as you curl up with your Bible, reading and declaring it, confidence in God's power and promises is being built. Knowing God's Word goes together with trusting Him and praying the Word over your life. Read the Word with the faith that it will come to pass, then pray the same words over your life. In God's Word lies strength, hope, peace, joy, love, and instructions to fight and be victorious over the enemy.

Furthermore, Christ has already won the victory for you through His death, burial, and resurrection. Now, you have ultimate victory over sin, death, and the devil. Colossians 2:15 AMPC says, *"[God] disarmed the principalities and powers that were ranged against us and made a bold display and public example of them, in triumphing over them in Him and in it [the cross]."* All you must do is dress and show up, standing on Christ's victory on the cross because He accomplished it for you. It's your victory, and now you operate and fight from it. It is your reality in Christ Jesus - know this, stand boldly in it, and walk in the spiritual authority the Cross of Christ has wrought for you.

Key Bible Verses for Victory

Christ has long established the believer's victory over sin, death, and the devil. One of the challenges to this truth is what Prophet Hosea said in Hosea 4:6, *"My people are destroyed for lack of knowledge."*

The Psalmist further highlighted this truth, *"They have neither knowledge nor understanding, they walk about in darkness; all the foundations of the earth are shaken. I said, 'You are gods, sons of the Most High, all of you.'"* - Psalms 82:5-6 ESV

The following Bible verses will help you recognize and remain in the victory of Christ:

Verses About God's Strength and Protection

When facing a daunting challenge and your strength is failing, or you require protection, these Bible verses will help you face your fears and surmount the impossible:

"The Lord is my light and my salvation- whom shall I fear? The Lord is the stronghold of my life, of whom shall I be afraid?" - Psalms 27:1

"God is our refuge and strength, an ever-present help in trouble." - Psalms 46:1

"No weapon forged against you will prevail, and you will refute every tongue that accuses you." - Isaiah 54:17

"But the Lord is faithful. He will establish you and guard you against the evil one." - 2 Thessalonians 3:3

"It is God who arms me with strength, and makes my way perfect." - Psalms 18:32

"Fear not, for I am with you; be not dismayed, for I am your God; I will strengthen you, I will help you, I will uphold you with my righteous right hand." - Isaiah 41:10

Verses Declaring Victory Over the Enemy

The enemy has no hold on you because Christ has given you victory through the following Bible verses:

"Submit yourselves, then, to God. Resist the devil, and he will flee from you." - James 4:7

"You, dear children, are from God and have overcome them because the one who is in you is greater than the one who is in the world." - 1 John 4:4

"The God of peace will soon crush Satan under your feet." - Romans 16:20

"But thanks be to God, who gives us the victory through our Lord Jesus Christ." - 1 Corinthians 15:57

"I have said these things to you, that in me you may have peace. In the world you will have tribulation. But take heart; I have overcome the world." - John 16:33

"The one who conquers, I will grant him to sit with me on my throne, as I also conquered and sat down with my Father on his throne." - Revelation 3:21

"For the LORD your God is he who goes with you to fight for you against your enemies, to give you the victory." - Deuteronomy 20:4

Verses to Build Faith and Courage

Challenges may appear overwhelming, making you lose heart and causing you to fear. In times like this, you can rest assured that God is with you – He never leaves.

Scriptural verses to solidify this truth in you are:

"Be strong and courageous. Do not be afraid, do not be discouraged, for the Lord your God will be with you wherever you go." - Joshua 1:9

"When I am afraid, I put my trust in you. In God, whose Word I praise, in God I trust and am not afraid." - Psalms 56:3-4

"For the Spirit God gave us does not make us timid, but gives us power, love, and self-discipline." - 2 Timothy 1:7

"God is our refuge and strength, an every-present help in trouble." - Psalms 46:1

"Be strong and courageous. Do not be afraid or terrified because of them, for the Lord your God goes with you; he will never leave you nor forsake you." - Deuteronomy 31:6

"Even though I walk through the valley of the shadow of death, I will fear no evil, for you are with me; your rod and your staff, they comfort me." - Psalms 23:4

Verses About Standing Firm in Faith

The call to stand firm is a scripture command repeated countless times.

A few are listed below:

"Finally, be strong in the Lord and his mighty power. Put on the full armor of God, so that you can take your stand against the devil's schemes." - Ephesians 6:10-11

"Therefore, my dear brothers and sisters, stand firm. Let nothing move you. Always give yourselves fully to the work of the Lord." - 1 Corinthians 15:58

"Stand firm, then, and do not let yourselves be burdened again by a yoke of slavery." - Galatians 5:1

"Be on the alert, stand firm in the faith, act like men, be strong." - 1 Corinthians 16:13

"But resist him, firm in your faith, knowing that the same experiences of suffering are being accomplished by your brethren who are in the world." - 1 Peter 5:9

"Conduct yourselves in a manner worthy of the gospel of Christ, so that whether I come and see you or remain absent, I will hear of you that you are standing firm in one spirit, with one mind striving together for the faith of the gospel." - Philippians 1:27

Verses About the Authority of Jesus and His Victory

Although the believer is in an ongoing spiritual warfare against the forces of darkness, Christ has already given them victory.

These verses attest to it:

"And having disarmed the powers and authorities, he made a public spectacle of them, triumphing over them by the cross." - Colossians 2:15

"But thanks be to God! He gives us the victory through our Lord Jesus Christ." - 1 Corinthians 15:57

"I have told you these things, so that in me you may have peace. In this world you will have trouble. But take heart! I have overcome the world." - John 16:33

"But thanks be to God, who in Christ always leads us in triumphal procession, and through us spreads the fragrance of the knowledge of him everywhere." - 2 Corinthians 2:14

"No, in all these things we are more than conquerors through him who loved us." - Romans 8:37

"Since, therefore, the children share in flesh and blood, he himself likewise partook of the same things, that through death he might destroy the one who has the power of death, that is, the devil." - Hebrews 2:14

Praying Scripture During Warfare

Praying during warfare becomes monotonous when believers don't know what to pray for, how to pray, or how to pray in their words, and there is no change. This has weakened many prayer lives. If you're in the same dilemma, ask yourself if you've tried praying scriptures.

Praying scriptures is praying God's Word to Him. It's using scripture to form the basis of your prayers. For instance, Jesus on the cross prayed Matthew 27:46 ESV, *"My God, my God, why have you forsaken me?"*

Why Should You Pray Scriptures During Warfare?

- **It teaches you what to pray.**

  Have you reached a point where you're tired of your regular prayer phrases, or do you feel your words are inadequate to communicate your mind? Praying God's Word gives you a fresh perspective on what to pray for. The beautiful thing about praying scripture is that the Word of God is *"sharper than any weapon, piercing into the heart of any attack of the enemy and* is a *discerner of the thoughts and intents of your heart."* - Hebrews 4:12. Whenever you pray God's Word, be sure of victory.

- **When you pray scripture, you align your request with God's will.**

  Instead of coming before God with a list of things you have figured out, a better way is to ask Him to help you not to "lean on your understanding" (Proverbs 3:5) and to guide you in searching for His "thoughts that are higher than yours" (Isaiah 55:9). This approach will completely change your prayer life and give you the assurance and peace that you've petitioned after His will – *"And this is the confidence that we have toward him, that if we ask anything according to his will, he hears us. And if we know that he hears us in whatever we ask, we know that we have the requests that we have asked of him."* - 1 John 5:14-15 ESV

- **Praying scriptures changes your heart's posture.**

    Reading the Bible from Genesis to Revelation reveals that God is very particular about man's heart, not what He gives to man. Once He gets you to where your heart's posture aligns with His will, He can use you mightily. Praying scriptures does this for you. The answer from praying scripture is often not what you had hoped for. For example, you ask God to heal your body. However, He's bringing to your mind a person you're bitter towards and urging you to forgive. When you choose God's answers over what you want, your heart shifts to trusting God more and being confident in your choices because you know where they came from. Also, your heart will be quick to hear God when He speaks because of its posture - leaning towards God and the manifestation of His will.

How to Pray Scriptures

If this is your first time hearing about praying through scriptures, the book of Psalms is the best place to begin. They're filled with David's discussions about his predicaments with the Lord.

Use this simple guide:

- Consider one of the Psalms or another Bible passage. Read it through, noting words you don't understand. Get a good Study Bible to help you comprehend what the passage entails.
- Go over the passage again, but this time slowly.
- Read it verse by verse, praying each verse that speaks to you. You must personalize the verse as you pray. Do not be in a hurry to jump to the next one. Milk each verse slowly until it dawns on you - *when you see yourself in each verse.* Worship, confess, rejoice, or shout if it's what the verse wants you to do. Be willing to engage with each verse as you read it.

For instance, while praying for protection, you declare, *"Lord, Your Word says no weapon formed against me shall prosper (Isaiah 54:17). I stand on this promise and declare Your protection over my life."*

Using Psalms 67 as a case study for passages with multiple verses, you could do this: read the passage and understand its words and meaning. Then, reread it slower, stopping periodically to pray.

Here it is:

"May God be gracious to us and bless us and make his face to shine upon us, Selah."

Lord, I bless your name. You are beautiful beyond description. For in You lie all things. As the Psalmist declares, Lord, I ask that You be gracious to me and my loved ones. Shine Your face upon us and show us Your Favor.

"That your way may be known on earth, your saving power among all nations."

Father, let Your name and the good news of salvation be known all over the Earth, with nations turning unto You.

"Let the peoples praise you, O God; let all the peoples praise you."

Lord, be praised in my life and my home. Let Your praise be heard in families, cities, and churches. (You can spend more time praying that your life and those connected to you would bring honor, praise, and glory to God; through your life, many lives would praise God.)

"Let the nations be glad and sing for joy, for you judge the peoples with equity and guide the nations upon the earth. Sela"

Lord, You have made me glad. Now I ask that the nations come to know You as a good God through my life, one who judges fairly and doesn't forsake.

"Let the peoples praise you, O God; let all the peoples praise you."

Lord, let my life sing forth Your praise and let it bring glory to You.

"The earth has yielded its increase; God, our God, shall bless us."

Lord, thank you for blessing me with increase and abundance. Yes, it's You who loads me daily with benefits. (Reflect on God's blessings upon your life, job, business, and loved ones)

"God shall bless us; let all the ends of the earth fear him!"

Lord, I see Your hands upon my life. You have blessed and will keep blessing me so that many will see this blessing and will fear and put their trust in You as a good Father.

The above illustration shows you how to pray with Scripture. You can do verse-by-verse like above, pick the central theme or the passage's meaning, and reword it in prayer to God. The beauty is that God's promise in Isaiah 55:11 ESV becomes a reality as you pray scripture - *"So shall my Word be that goes out from my mouth; it shall not return to me empty, but it shall accomplish that which I purpose and shall succeed in the thing for which I sent it."*

Creating a Scripture Arsenal

A soldier doesn't prepare for war when it's already brewing close. Instead, preparations like physical and mental training, logistical and equipment planning, operational planning, and evaluation were carried out long before the first shot was fired. In other words, soldiers live ready for combat. It is the same for the believer - don't wait for the enemy to drop a bomb before you're in a war zone. There's a real and ongoing spiritual warfare, and your scripture arsenal must be ready to defend against the enemy's attacks. Therefore, create a list of your favorite warfare verses (offensive and defensive) and keep it close for easy access during times of trouble, for it will surely come. Ask the Holy Spirit to open your mind and heart to understand the Word before you study.

As believers, the Word of God is your weapon. It *"is living and active, sharper than any two-edged sword, piercing to the division of soul and of spirit, of joints and of marrow, and discerning the thoughts and intentions of the heart."* - Hebrews 4:12 ESV. It's the believer's ultimate weapon against the enemy's lies and attacks. The only offensive weapon in the armor of God is the sword, according to Ephesians 6:17, *"And take the helmet of salvation, and the sword of the Spirit, which is the Word of God."* It was not designed to attack people; it was to defend against and defeat the enemy and be a source of strength and guidance for the believer. For instance, Jesus, who is God and man, overcame the enemy's temptation in the wilderness by declaring the Word (Matthew 4:1-11). He set the precedent for believers when combating the enemy's lies and schemes. For more on this subject, refer to the book <u>Spiritual Warfare.</u>

Chapter 5: Quotes of Faith and Encouragement

Words are potent - they show the state of your mind and reveal to others your personality. Words can heal, bring life or death, and build or destroy relationships, depending on how you use them. You should always speak words founded in God's truth and promises to shape your life and destiny because words spoken are like spiritual seeds sown.

The words from the Bible are more effective than you know.[15]

No surprise, the Bible states:

"Death and life are in the power of the tongue, and those who love it will eat its fruit." - Proverbs 18:21 NKJV

As a believer, your words (confessions) are powerful and matter immensely. You must understand that when you confess positive words deeply rooted in Biblical principles, God's truth and promises turn situations around, strengthening and healing you. God's Word (the scriptures) encourages and fortifies you for spiritual warfare against the enemy. The scriptures are forever living and active to guide you through life's challenges and obstacles.

"For the Word of God is living and powerful, and sharper than any two-edged sword, piercing even to the division of soul and spirit, and of joints and marrow, and is a discerner of the thoughts and intents of the heart." - Hebrews 4:12 NKJV

"For whatever was written in earlier times was written for our instruction, so that through endurance and the encouragement of the Scriptures we might have hope and overflow with confidence in His promises." - Romans 15:4 AMP

Apostle Paul's message explained that your hope and confidence are based on God's Word. The scripture was written for you to read, believe, and speak over your life, to receive strength and hope in times of weakness, and to make life easier.

This living Word of God helps you stand firm in defeating the enemy in spiritual warfare. You can rely on God's Word because once He speaks, He will commit. *"For You have magnified Your Word above all Your name."* - Psalms 138:2b NKJV.

Therefore, encourage yourself in the Lord and trust His promises, which are true and always come to pass.

"Not a word failed of any good thing which the Lord had spoken to the house of Israel. All came to pass." - Joshua 21:45 NKJV

God's Word teaches you what to do in every situation. If you forsake worldly wisdom and believe His Word and promises for guidance, help, and strength, be assured of victory. His words encourage you to have a great life, build you up, and make you a believer ready to overcome spiritual warfare and tough times to enjoy an abundant life.

"Trust in the Lord with all your heart, and lean not on your own understanding; In all your ways acknowledge Him, and He shall direct

your paths. Do not be wise in your own eyes; Fear the Lord and depart from evil." - Proverbs 3:5-7 NKJV

How to Use Scriptures for Encouragement

The scriptures help build courage in the believer. Scriptures to encourage yourself are:

Strengthening Your Faith: The scriptures are God's Word written to strengthen your faith in Him. Reading them reminds you of His presence, power, and faithfulness, even in overwhelming circumstances.

"Fear not, for I am with you; Be not dismayed, for I am your God. I will strengthen you, yes, I will help you, I will uphold you with My righteous right hand." - Isaiah 41:10 NKJV

Encourages Perseverance: God's Word gives you the endurance you need to keep going through the trials and temptations of life without giving in and losing hope.

"Blessed is the man who endures temptation; for when he has been approved, he will receive the crown of life which the Lord has promised to those who love Him." - James 1:12 NKJV

Your spirit is strengthened when you believe and declare God's Word in your downtimes. You can press on to victory with this strength and your faith in God intact.

"Consider it nothing but joy, my brothers and sisters, whenever you fall into various trials. Be assured that the testing of your faith [through experience] produces endurance [leading to spiritual maturity, and inner peace]. And let endurance have its perfect result and do a thorough work, so that you may be perfect and completely developed [in your faith], lacking in nothing." - James 1:2-4 AMP

Aligning Your Perspective with God's Promises: The Bible constantly encourages you to see challenges through God's eternal plan and to trust Him fully. When you face a difficult circumstance, instead of succumbing to fear, turn to God's Word and promises in the scriptures and align your heart in His direction. The scriptures are packed with God's plans and promises for His Children. Let these be your encouragement and response to the enemy's lies.

"For I know the thoughts that I think toward you, says the Lord, thoughts of peace and not of evil, to give you a future and a hope. Then you will call upon Me and go and pray to Me, and I will listen to you.

And you will seek Me and find Me when you search for Me with all your heart." -Jeremiah 29:11-13 NKJV

"And we know that all things work together for good to those who love God, to those who are the called according to His purpose." - Romans 8:28 NKJV

Key Themes and Bible Verses for Encouragement

Provided that you are in this world, the enemy will always throw shade at you. The Word of God is the only thing that keeps you from falling into the enemy's trap.

Bible verses broken into several themes to help you stand firm in the circumstances are:

Trusting God in Uncertainty

Amid uncertainty and confusion, when things are not clear, remember that God is with you. Refer to His words in the scriptures for comfort, and trust them to guide you rightly.

"Trust in the Lord with all your heart, and lean not on your own understanding; In all your ways acknowledge Him, and He shall direct your paths."- Proverbs 3:5-6 NKJV

The scripture explains that if you trust the Lord, He will lead you out of uncertainty, chaos, and confusion.

"For I know the thoughts that I think toward you, says the Lord, thoughts of peace and not of evil, to give you a future and a hope." - Jeremiah 29:11 NKJV

As part of God's family, He has good plans and thoughts for you. You only need to trust Him entirely and expect the best outcome.

"Commit your way to the Lord, trust also in Him, and He shall bring it to pass." - Psalms 37:5 NKJV

The scripture shows that when you put all your plans (present and future) in God's hands, He will make great things happen.

"The fear of man brings a snare, but whoever trusts in and puts his confidence in the Lord will be exalted and safe." - Proverbs 29:25 KJV

The scripture clearly states that man's fear, uncertainty, and chaos would bring continual bondage and more fear. However, when you put your trust and confidence in God, you are safe and exalted above the uncertainty and chaos. So, learn always to put your trust in God, no matter the circumstances.

Prayer: Amid uncertainty, say this prayer of trust in God: *"Heavenly Father, in moments of doubt and fear, I choose to trust in You. Your Word promises that You have plans for my good, and You will direct my steps. Strengthen my faith to rely fully on Your wisdom. In Jesus' name, Amen."*

Overcoming Fear and Doubt

As a believer, at any given time, you can always overcome fear and doubt with the Word of God firmly rooted in your heart. Consider these Bible verses to boost your faith to face fears and doubt:

"Fear not, for I am with you; Be not dismayed, for I am your God. I will strengthen you, yes, I will help you, I will uphold you with My righteous right hand." - Isaiah 41:10 NKJV

In this scripture, you're urged to remain unafraid regardless of the situation because God's divine presence is always with you. He will comfort and guide you through difficult situations. Speak His words, believe and trust in His promises, and watch fear and doubt give way.

"For God has not given us a spirit of fear, but of power and of love and of a sound mind." - 2 Timothy 1:7 NKJV

God expects you to cast away fear and act boldly in situations because He has given you a bold and sound mind. Hence, you can withstand any challenge and stand victorious in spiritual warfare.

"Whenever I am afraid, I will trust in You. In God (I will praise His Word), In God I have put my trust; I will not fear. What can flesh do to me?" - Psalms 56:3-4

The Psalmist said he overcame fear and doubt because He trusted God. Equally, why should you be afraid? If your trust is in God's Word, you can overcome fear and doubt, and no situation can overwhelm you.

"Even though I walk through the [sunless] valley of the shadow of death, I fear no evil, for You are with me; Your rod [to protect] and Your staff [to guide], they comfort and console me." - Psalms 23:4 AMP

The Psalmist says that the Lord protects him in tough situations, like the valley of the shadow of death, which is enough to make anyone shiver in fear. This connotes that, regardless of the situation, remember that the Lord is with you. His protective rod and staff - His Word and His presence - are enough for you to overcome fear and doubt to scale through tough times unscathed.

Prayer: *"Lord, I surrender my fears, for You have not given me a spirit of fear, but of power, love, and a sound mind. Fill me with courage and remind me that You are always with me. In Jesus' name, Amen."*

Finding Strength in Trials

Life will always throw trials and temptations your way. However, you must find strength in these times and keep pushing. How do you find strength? By relying on and believing in God's Word, His promises, and obeying.

Consider these Bible verses on how you can draw strength during times of trials:

"I can do all things through Christ who strengthens me." - Philippians. 4:13 NKJV

You can do almost anything you set your mind to by the power of Christ in you, which gives you the strength to push on and be excellent at any task. When you believe this, things will work out for you.

"I have told you these things, so that in Me you may have [perfect] peace. In the world, you have tribulation and distress and suffering, but be courageous [be confident, be undaunted, be filled with joy]; I have overcome the world. [My conquest is accomplished, My victory abiding.]" - John 16:33 (AMP)

God already knows that believers will face trials and temptations, so He made provisions to live victoriously by giving His son (His Word). Faith in the Son is the only way to conquer trials without worrying about them.

"But those who wait on the Lord shall renew their strength; They shall mount up with wings like eagles, they shall run and not be weary, they shall walk and not faint." - Isaiah 40:31 NKJV

Waiting on the Lord is one way to find strength during trials and temptations. When you wait on the Lord through fasting and praying or reading and meditating on His Word, you get renewed, refreshed, and empowered to overcome numerous life challenges and obstacles.

"My brethren, count it all joy when you fall into various trials, knowing that the testing of your faith produces patience. But let patience have its perfect work, that you may be perfect and complete, lacking nothing." - James 1:2-4 NKJV

The Bible says you should be happy and encouraged in trials because they test your faith, strengthening you in the long run. See these trials as stepping stones to greatness and increased faith in God.

Prayer: *"Father, I feel weak, but I know your strength is made perfect in my weakness. Renew my spirit and help me to stand firm in faith, trusting that you are refining me through this trial. In Jesus' name, Amen."*

Faith and Hope for the Future

There is hope for a bright future when you can boldly speak God's Word into your life. Believe and hold on to every promise in faith while speaking it into your future. Speak the Word into your future, and you will see it manifest.

When you speak the Lord's Words into your heart, you can begin to feel faith and hope for the future.[16]

The scriptures below confirm this:

"Let us hold fast the confession of our hope without wavering, for He who promised is faithful." - Hebrews 10:23 NKJV

No future comes by chance. You are responsible for your future's outcome. One way to build your desired future is through your words. A Godly confession of hope and favorable things will manifest because God is faithful to bring them to pass.

"And we know that all things work together for good to those who love God, to those who are the called according to His purpose." Romans 8:28 (NKJV)

Whatever happens to a believer should be viewed as part of God's plan for a prosperous future and an expected end. Trust Him completely to convert everything (good and bad) in your favor. So long as you trust in Him, believe His Word, and confess it boldly, He will perfect everything concerning you and your future.

"Now hope does not disappoint, because the love of God has been poured out in our hearts by the Holy Spirit who was given to us." - Romans 5:5 NKJV

Hope and faith in God are essential for an excellent future because God doesn't disappoint His children. He has given you His love and Holy Spirit to comfort and guide your life.

"You are my hiding place and my shield; I hope in Your Word." - Psalms 119:114 NKJV

Your faith in God makes the difference and shields you from the enemy's attack. Believe that your future is secured and no situation can overwhelm you because God is your hiding place, from whom you draw strength, and have placed all your trust in Him.

Prayer: As you keep your faith in God and hope for your future alive, say this prayer of faith and hope: *"Lord, my hope is in You, even when I do not see the full picture. I trust that You are working all things for my good. Strengthen my faith so I may stand firm in hope, knowing that You are always faithful. In Jesus' name, Amen."*

Triumphing Over Sickness and Infirmities

Sickness and disease are not a part of God's plan for you. Therefore, God wants you to triumph over it by believing in His son, Jesus Christ, who took upon Himself your infirmities.

"He was beaten so we could be whole. He was whipped so we could be healed." - Isaiah 53:5b NLT

"Then He healed many who were sick with various diseases, and cast out many demons; and He did not allow the demons to speak, because they knew Him." - Mark 1:34 NKJV

When Jesus was on Earth, he healed those who believed in Him. However, when He died, He took sickness away from those who believe in Him, and now, when the enemy throws sickness and infirmities at you, remind him of God's gift of health to His children via the cross.

"Wherever He entered, into villages, cities, or the country, they laid the sick in the marketplaces, and begged Him that they might just touch the hem of His garment. And as many as touched Him were made well." - Mark 6:56 NKJV

"He sent His Word and healed them, and rescued them from their destruction." - Psalms 107:20 AMP

As this scripture says, God's Word to heal you from illnesses and infirmities is timely. His words are powerful to heal if you believe and have faith.

"Is anyone among you sick? Let him call for the elders of the church, and let them pray over him, anointing him with oil in the name of the Lord. And the prayer of faith will save the sick, and the Lord will raise him up. And if he has committed sins, he will be forgiven." - James 5:14-15 NKJV

The Bible talks about the role of your spiritual leaders to help you overcome sickness and infirmities. You are encouraged to meet them to pray for you; with faith in God, you will be healed.

Prayer: *"Lord, I trust you for healing my sicknesses and infirmities. I believe Christ has paid it all for me to be whole again. I walk in His victory over death, sicknesses, and infirmities. In Jesus' name, Amen."*

Prayers become effective when you actively speak and engage the powerful Word of God. His Word answers a situation in the mouth of believers. Therefore, you should understand that your faith in His Word must supersede circumstances to see victory. Always pray, keep declaring God's words over your life, constantly proclaim His promises over situations, and see yourself overcoming the enemy and winning life's battles.

Chapter 6: Prayers For Specific Spiritual Attacks

The enemy attacks believers in no particular way. His attacks against you can come in various forms like fear, anxiety, doubt, discouragement, temptation, confusion, and many other ways. But it shouldn't scare you or make you forget Christ won you the victory. Instead, be more conscious that God has empowered you with weapons to fight back whenever the enemy attacks. These weapons are readily available as fervent prayers, studying scriptures, strong faith in God, and complete reliance on the Holy Spirit.

Spiritual attacks can be taken care of with certain prayers.[17]

"The weapons of our warfare are not physical [weapons of flesh and blood]. Our weapons are divinely powerful for the destruction of fortresses. We are destroying sophisticated arguments and every exalted and proud thing that sets itself up against the [true] knowledge of God, and we are taking every thought and purpose captive to the obedience of Christ." - 2 Corinthians 10:4-5 AMP

Apostle Paul told the Christians in Corinth that the weapons God gave them to fight the enemy were not the physical weapons they were used to seeing because the battle (spiritual warfare) and the enemy to be conquered wasn't a physical one, so no physical weapon was needed. So, if you know and fully understand these weapons: praying in the Spirit, reading God's Word, holding firm in your faith in God, and relying entirely on the Holy Spirit for help and reawakening, you can effectively use them to defeat the enemy in spiritual warfare.

With these, you can view trials not as defeat but as great opportunities to demonstrate and grow your trust in God and His power to save.

"Consider it nothing but joy, my brothers and sisters, whenever you fall into various trials. Be assured that the testing of your faith [through experience] produces endurance [leading to spiritual maturity, and inner peace]. And let endurance have its perfect result and do a thorough work, so that you may be perfect and completely developed [in your faith], lacking in nothing." -James 1:2-4 AMP

The scripture says that you must remain joyful when the enemy attacks with trials and temptations because it builds your faith in God and strengthens and molds you into the perfect believer God wants you to be. Therefore, you must remain firm and unshaken when the enemy attacks your mind or emotions because the enemy knows that many believers are heavily controlled by their emotions. He is not after your expensive car or jewelry; he doesn't care about the money in your account, your mansion, your gold wristwatch, or your assets. He only cares about attacking you to make you doubt God's goodness and power over your life.

You may have heard Christian leaders say the devil has no power. You may be wondering, how does he attack the believer's mindset and emotions in spiritual warfare? He manipulates your emotions by tempting you with varying trials, deceiving you, making you unnecessarily anxious, fearful, confused, or attacking your finances, children, money, business, academics, or anything dear to you. His only aim is to push you to live a life of unbelief and doubt God's power, which is not part of God's plan and purpose for you.

"Yet in all these things we are more than conquerors through Him who loved us."-Romans 8:37 AMP

This chapter explores a few scriptures on properly praying against the devil's attacks on your emotions.

Prayers Against Fear and Anxiety

"For God has not given us a spirit of fear, but of power and of love and of a sound mind." - 2 Timothy 1:7 NKJV

One significant way the enemy attacks your emotions is through fear and anxiety. The devil will do everything to constantly remind you of the bad situations around you, to make you doubt God and what He has done in your life, and gradually push your mind into a state of unnecessary fear and anxiety. The Bible tells you that God has given you the spirit of power, love, and a sound mind. Fear is not a part of God's package for His children, so you need not fear, no matter the situation or the enemy's claims. When the devil is trying to make you anxious, endeavor always to fix your mind steadily on God's goodness, His faithfulness, and the finished work of Christ on the cross.

"Do not be anxious or worried about anything, but in everything [every circumstance and situation] by prayer and petition with thanksgiving, continue to make your [specific] requests known to God. And the peace of God [that peace which reassures the heart, that peace] which transcends all understanding, [that peace which] stands guard over your hearts and your minds in Christ Jesus [is yours]." - Philippians 4:6-7 AMP

The scriptures say you shouldn't be worried about anything; your finances that took a hit, your car broke down, your bills are due, your child is sick; whatever the situation, God's Word tells you not to worry and panic. Everything is under control when your faith and belief in God are strong. You only need to pray and give thanks to God because He is always with you. He has given you His Word to comfort, guide, and strengthen you even when the enemy attacks you with fear and anxiety.

"Do not fear [anything], for I am with you; Do not be afraid, for I am your God. I will strengthen you, be assured I will help you; I will certainly take hold of you with My righteous right hand [a hand of justice, of power, of victory, of salvation]." - Isaiah 41:10 AMP

"Casting all your cares [all your anxieties, all your worries, and all your concerns, once and for all] on Him, for He cares about you [with deepest affection, and watches over you very carefully]." - 1 Peter 5:7 AMP

You are encouraged to cast away fear because your Father God cares so much about you. He sees what you are going through and makes provisions for your victory. So, you don't fear or worry about how you will handle the situation, which keeps you awake all night. God cares for you. If your earthly father cares so much for you, how much more does your Heavenly God, who will give you anything you ask of Him (Matthew 7:11).

"Peace I leave with you; My [perfect] peace I give to you; not as the world gives do I give to you. Do not let your heart be troubled, nor let it be afraid. [Let My perfect peace calm you in every circumstance and give you courage and strength for every challenge.]" -John 14:27 AMP

God has given believers His peace in this world full of troubles, trials, and tribulations. His peace calms every fiery dart from the adversary, the devil. God says you shouldn't be bothered or fear anything. You should be confident and fearless in the face of the enemy's attack because your mind is completely fixed on God's Word and His promises. The peace He has given you surpasses any situation or circumstance if you believe.

Prayer: Say this prayer of faith in God during anxiety and fear: *"Heavenly Father, I surrender my fears to You. Your Word says You have not given me a spirit of fear, but of power, love, and a sound mind. I refuse to let fear control me. Strengthen me with Your peace and remind me that You are always with me. I put my trust in You, Lord, for You are my refuge and strength. In Jesus' name, Amen."*

Prayer for Strength Against Temptation

"No temptation [regardless of its source] has overtaken or enticed you that is not common to human experience [nor is any temptation unusual or beyond human resistance]; but God is faithful [to His Word - He is compassionate and trustworthy], and He will not let you be tempted beyond your ability [to resist], but along with the temptation He [has in the past and is now and] will [always] provide the way out as well, so that you will be able to endure it [without yielding, and will overcome temptation with joy]." - 1 Corinthians 10:13 AMP

The Bible has categorically stated that there is no temptation greater than the power God has given you to overcome it. He will not allow temptation that is greater than you. So, you must trust His Word fully and believe it has everything for you to walk in righteousness and defeat the enemy's temptations.

"Awake to righteousness, and do not sin." - 1 Corinthians 15:34a NKJV

When you accept and believe in Christ's finished work on the cross, living a righteous life by being more conscious that you are now a child of God becomes easier. This consciousness is achieved by actively reading the Word of God (sword of the spirit), constantly keeping or surrounding yourself with what edifies your mind and spirit, and continuously praying to God for strength to overcome the enemy's temptations.

"Keep away from everything that even looks like sin." - 1 Thessalonians 5:22 NLV

When you are more conscious of your righteous state in Christ, you refrain from anything that looks like sin, as God's Word commands. Temptations are no longer a problem to overcome.

Prayer: *"Lord, I am weak, but You are strong. You promised to provide a way out of every temptation. Help me to turn away from sin and walk in righteousness. Fill me with Your Spirit, so I can resist what is not from You. I declare victory over temptation in the name of Jesus, Amen."*

Prayer Against Spiritual Confusion and Deception

"For God is not the author of confusion but of peace, as in all the churches of the saints." - 1 Corinthians 14:33 NKJV

Confusion does not originate from God. The scriptures state that He is a God of peace. Your adversary, the devil, is the culprit of confusion; he seeks those he can deceive with his manipulations, tricks, and lies. You, the believer, must guard your heart and mind with the powerful truth of God's Word, stand firm in it, and discard the devil's lies. He uses these lies to confuse and deceive you because he knows that discouragement, fear, and anxiety set in when you are confused, and unbelief surfaces.

Therefore, you must rely on the Holy Spirit for the grace to discern spiritual confusion, pray to God for the wisdom to act accordingly, stand firm in your faith, believe the scriptures concerning your life and destiny, believe the promises of God for your life and family, and pray fervently against deception and confusion. Even if the enemy tries to deceive and lie to you, you have a weapon to fight him because you are well-grounded in the truth of God's Word. You can boldly proclaim the scripture in Psalms 118:17 NKJV, *"I shall not die, but live, and declare the works of the Lord."*

When the devil tries to confuse and make you feel like you are unloved by God or you are not a candidate for God's kingdom, you immediately know you can boldly say you are the righteousness of God in Christ Jesus. This is true because you are a new creature believing in His finished work on the cross and reign with Him.

"For He made Him who knew no sin to be sin for us, that we might become the righteousness of God in Him." - 2 Corinthians 5:21 NKJV

"The righteousness of God through faith in Jesus Christ for all who believe. For there is no distinction." - Romans 3:22 ESV

You can counter the devil with God's Word when the enemy tries to convince you that you are under invisible spiritual chains and curses.

"Christ has redeemed us from the curse of the law, having become a curse for us, for it is written, 'Cursed is everyone who hangs on a tree.'" - Galatians 3:13 NKJV

"No weapon formed against you shall prosper, and every tongue which rises against you in judgment, you shall condemn. This is the heritage of the servants of the Lord, and their righteousness is from Me," Says the Lord." - Isaiah 54:17 (NKJV)

Prayer: You can better overcome deception and confusion with this daily prayer: *"Heavenly Father, when my mind feels clouded and I struggle to discern the truth, remind me that You are a God of peace, not confusion. Fill me with wisdom and clarity through Your Holy Spirit. Guard my heart and mind against deception and lead me in Your truth. In Jesus' name, Amen."*

Prayers Against Sickness and Spiritual Weakness

"But He has said to me, "My grace is sufficient for you [My lovingkindness and My mercy are more than enough - always available - regardless of the situation]; for [My] power is being perfected [and is completed and shows itself most effectively] in [your] weakness." Therefore, I will all the more gladly boast in my weaknesses, so that the power of Christ [may completely enfold me and] may dwell in me." - 2 Corinthians 12:9 AMP

"Beloved, I pray that in every way you may succeed and prosper and be in good health [physically], just as [I know] your soul prospers [spiritually]." - 3 John 1:2 (AMP)

"He sent out his Word and healed them; he rescued them from the grave." - Psalms 107:20 NIV

"But He was wounded for our transgressions, He was bruised for our iniquities; The chastisement for our peace was upon Him, and by His stripes we are healed." - Isaiah 53:5 NKJV

"You shall serve [only] the Lord your God, and He shall bless your bread and water. I will also remove sickness from among you." - Exodus 23:25 AMP

God has not given us the spirit of fear, but of power, love, and a sound mind. In the same way, He has not destined His children to suffer illnesses and infirmities. The scripture says God wants you to be in good health, and even as your soul prospers, He will restore your health and take sickness and disease away from you and your family. It says you are healed by the stripes of Jesus Christ, who died on the cross for the sins of the world. These clearly indicate that God is invested in your health and spiritual strength as a believer. He gave His Word to heal you and give you the strength to stand firm when the enemy attacks you with sickness. Sickness is an attack from the enemy; he is the author of discomfort and pain. But the believer is encouraged to take hold of God's Word, "The Truth and the Life." Firmly believing God's Word gives you life from within, and believing that he has already healed you from sickness and made you victorious strengthens you even more to fight back and stand firm in the enemy's attacks.

"Lord, by such things people live; and my spirit finds life in them too. You restored me to health and let me live. Surely it was for my benefit that I suffered such anguish. In your love, you kept me from the pit of destruction; you have put all my sins behind your back." - Isaiah 38:16-17 NIV

Sometimes, everything seems to be down for a believer; the enemy manipulates and tries to make you believe you are nothing. He will continually remind you of your sins and bad situations around you. The Bible calls him the accuser of the brethren. The enemy's primary aim is to quench your belief in God by attacking you with sickness and spiritual weakness. He hopes to affect your faith and prayer life if you are not firmly rooted in God's Word and His promises. However, if you are firmly rooted in God's Word, you read and believe His Word and every promise, declare prayers that are strongly backed by the scriptures, and understand your place in Christ (the believer's authority), the devil will fail in making you feel less of yourself.

Therefore, when you feel cloudiness, uncertainty, or weakness in your spirit, when you think you can't do anything to fulfill your destiny, remember what the scriptures say:

"I can do all things through Christ who strengthens me." - Philippians 4:13 NKJV

Prayer: Say this prayer daily for healing and strength: *"Lord, I believe in Your Word that says You will take sickness and infirmities from me, I pray and believe that You have strengthened me when I was weak and overwhelmed by circumstances; thank you, Father, for all You have done for me. In Jesus' name, Amen."*

Prayers Against Financial Attacks

"Beloved, I pray that in every way you may succeed and prosper and be in good health [physically], just as [I know] your soul prospers [spiritually]." - 3 John 1:2 AMP

"The blessing of the Lord brings [true] riches, and He adds no sorrow to it [for it comes as a blessing from God]." - Proverbs. 10:22 AMP

"The thief comes only in order to steal and kill and destroy. I came that they may have and enjoy life, and have it in abundance [to the full, till it overflows]." - John 10:10 AMP

The scriptures clearly show the mind of your Heavenly Father towards your finances. He doesn't want His children to be poor or needy. Like you eagerly aim for financial freedom and success, God also wants it for you. His plan is for you to live a life of abundance and prosperity. So, when your adversary, the devil, tries to attack your finances with unnecessary setbacks and losses (because he will), the truth of God's Word in the scriptures will help you overcome him.

Your faith in His Word matters because the enemy constantly lies and deceives you. Instead of giving in to his attacks, ignore him, keep working diligently, and pray scripture-based prayers. Also, since you know God wishes for your finances, keep declaring His Word in fervent prayers over your financial situation.

"For I know the plans I have for you," declares the Lord, "plans to prosper you and not to harm you, plans to give you hope and a future." - Jeremiah 29:11 NIV

"But remember the Lord your God, for it is he who gives you the ability to produce wealth, and so confirms his covenant, which he swore to your ancestors, as it is today." - Deuteronomy 8:18 NIV

God gives you the wisdom, ability, strength, and power to make wealth, not your ability or power. So, ask for His wisdom, divine provision, and strength to make wealth and grow your finances. While praying, you must strongly resist the devil's influence over your finances. Continuously stand on God's Word and His promises, believe them, and you will see them come to pass in your finances.

"And my God will liberally supply (fill until full) your every need according to His riches in glory in Christ Jesus." - Philippians 4:19 NIV

"Jabez cried out to the God of Israel, "Oh, that you would bless me and enlarge my territory! Let your hand be with me, and keep me from harm so that I will be free from pain." And God granted his request." - 1 Chronicles 4:10 NIV

This passage proves that God cares and wants you to be financially buoyant. It shows that He answers His children's financial prayers. Jabez earnestly prayed to God for success, and God heard him. Your faith must remain firm in God, even during trying times and financial setbacks, because the enemy aims to push you into unbelief.

Prayer: Say this prayer daily as you seek financial success while overcoming the enemy's attack on your finances: *"Father, I know and thank You for the good thoughts You have towards my finances, and for*

the provisions and numerous blessings You have made available. I ask for Your wisdom and strength to make wealth and grow financially. I command the enemy to get his hands off my finances. In Jesus' name, Amen."

These are simple but powerful steps and prayers to follow. Add these prayers to your prayer journals. However, you are not restricted to these prayers; add your own prayers in the box provided below:

The area(s) I feel spiritually attacked:

1. _____
2. _____
3. _____

Scriptures that explain my victory from these attacks (search the scriptures, highlighted passages in the book, or online to guide you).

1. _____
2. _____
3. _____

Prayer (write down your prayers, using the knowledge from your researched scriptures to claim your victory)

_____
_____
_____
_____
_____
_____
_____

Remember, as a believer, you can stand firm in the enemy's attacks because you have been adequately equipped with the spiritual weapon of God's Word (the sword of the Spirit). By relying entirely on God's Word and His Holy Spirit, you draw enough strength, wisdom, and courage to overcome fears of the unknown, doubts, anxiety, confusion, and temptations from the enemy. With a better understanding, say your daily prayers, backing them by declaring these powerful scriptures. Be assured that you are victorious through Christ.

Chapter 7: Prayers for Protection and Deliverance

During trials, challenges, and evil looming worldwide, people ask questions like: Does God protect His people? Does he care? Would he show up and save the day? Most times, these questions arise from confusion and helplessness. However, based on Christian beliefs, God's protection and deliverance are firmly founded on the conviction that God is a loving and merciful creator, a shield and fortress for His people in their troubles. The Bible has several instances of the need for protection and deliverance from distress, danger, or uncertainty and why you should pray for them. Even Jesus, while teaching His disciples how to pray, taught them to pray in this manner: *"And lead us not into temptation, but deliver us from evil."* - Matthew 6:13 ESV

There are prayers for protection you need to always remember.[18]

Protection refers to God's safeguarding from harm. It goes beyond God merely shielding you from danger to Him providing you with strength, assurance, and guidance in every situation. Deliverance is God's power to rescue you from danger, oppression, sin, and spiritual attacks. It's rooted in Jesus Christ's authority, who defeated the powers of darkness through His death and resurrection (Colossians 2:15).

Since prayer is powerful for protecting yourself and your loved ones and breaking free from the enemy's grip, this chapter explores biblical prayer for protection and deliverance and provides useful tips for pursuing and experiencing its benefits.

Strongholds

Stronghold in the Christian space may seem like a buzzword, but it's far from it. It has different biblical representations, as seen in Psalms 9:9, where it's a defensive structure: *"The Lord is a stronghold for the oppressed, a stronghold in times of trouble"* ESV. It could be regarded as a hiding place, as seen in 1 Samuel 23:14 ESV, *"And David remained in the strongholds in the wilderness, in the hill country of the wilderness of Ziph. And Saul sought him every day, but God did not give him into his hand."*

However, it's represented in this chapter as patterns of thought, sin, or oppression that hold believers captive. These thoughts become habitual, forming a pattern built into your life to keep you bound. They affect your relationship with God and hinder you from living your destined lives in God. Equally, they keep believers at the enemy's mercy.

It's established that your presence in this world means that you're in a war zone. This war is not fought with guns, knives, sticks, or anything physical because the battle is waged in your mind. The enemy and his agents are particular about attacking your mind because it's the citadel of your soul. The Apostle Paul likened it this way, *"For those who live according to the flesh set their minds on the things of the flesh, but those who live according to the Spirit set their minds on the things of the Spirit. For to set the mind on the flesh is death, but to set the mind on the Spirit is life and peace."* - Romans 8:5-6 ESV

Spiritual strongholds restrict you from clear reasoning and accepting the truth of God's Word. It keeps you in a rut of repeated failure, mistakes, and lies. So, how do you take down spiritual strongholds? 2 Corinthians 10:3-5 ESV gives the clue: *"For though we walk in the flesh,* we are not waging war according to the flesh. For the weapons of our warfare are not of the flesh but have divine power to destroy strongholds. We destroy arguments and every lofty opinion raised against the knowledge of God, and take every thought captive to obey Christ."

This scripture explains that the first step is to recognize the stronghold and then activate deliverance prayers to break free from its chains.

What Can Prevent Deliverance?

There are two sides to every notable deliverance – God's and yours. The good news is that God has fulfilled His part already. Now, it depends on you to fulfill yours. Deliverance begins when you close the door to the devil, turn away from sin, and surrender your soul fully to God. How can you achieve this?

Recognize Your Need for Deliverance: You can't fight a battle you're unaware of or an enemy you don't know. When realizing an area you need deliverance over, the Holy Spirit helps you.

Repent and Renounce: Ask God to reveal anything in you that needs to come to light. True repentance goes beyond confessing; it's brokenness, coming before God with a contrite heart, and turning away from sin. You verbally confess your sin, renouncing anything that's not of God you might have gotten involved with, completely shutting the door to them. *"If we confess our sins, he is faithful and just and will forgive us our sins and purify us from all unrighteousness."* - 1 John 1:9

Release Yourself and Resist the Enemy: Praying in the name of Jesus carries authority and power to break the enemy's hold. *"And these signs will accompany those who believe, in my name they will drive out demons."* - Mark 16:17. Release yourself in the name of Jesus from every satanic hold. For instance, say I release myself from the spirit of depression, heaviness, pornography, etc. Ensure you stand your ground, resisting (James 4:7) when the enemy comes back with sweeter deals to lure you into what you were just released from.

Replace and Renew Your Mind: The flesh is always desirous of things outside the will of God, which is why the enemy always encourages you to feed it with its desires. Deliverance comes when you consciously feed the Spirit and starve the flesh of its desires. The Christian walk doesn't end with accepting Christ as Lord; this is the first step. Afterward, with the holy spirit's help, you're expected to fill your mind with Scriptures (God's Word). When you do, you'll see yourself in the light of your new identity (2 Corinthians 5:17) to easily spot the enemy's lies and replace them with the truth of God's Word. Only then can you walk in Christ's dominion.

Find a Bible-Believing Church and Stay There: Belonging and participating among a body of believers will nourish, encourage and support your Christian walk. The enemy's easy prey are the lone wolves, but when in the park (body of believers), it becomes a challenge for him to get to you.

Key Scriptures for Deliverance Prayers

Deliverance prayer is vital for healing. This healing could be spiritual, physical, or emotional. Through scriptures, you gain an understanding of Satan's existence and his evil schemes and how Christ has wrought the victory for you.

Scriptures for deliverance prayers to buttress your dominion over the enemy are:

God's Deliverance Promise

The Bible is full of God's precious promises of deliverance. Since His Word always prevails, you can fill your heart with these promises.

"The righteous cry out and the Lord hears them, he delivers them from all their troubles." - Psalms 34:17

"Call upon me in the day of trouble, I will deliver you, and you shall glorify me." - Psalms 50:15

"And the LORD shall deliver me from every evil work and will preserve me unto His Heavenly Kingdom: to Whom be glory forever and ever. Amen." - 2 Timothy 4:18

"And it shall come to pass, that whosoever shall call on the Name of the LORD shall be delivered: for in mount Zion and in Jerusalem shall be deliverance, as the LORD hath said, and in the remnant whom the LORD shall call." - Joel 2:32

"But we had the sentence of death in ourselves, that we should not trust in ourselves, but in God which raiseth the dead: Who delivered us from so great a death, and doth deliver: in Whom we trust that He will yet deliver us." - 2 Corinthians 1:9-10

"Who gave Himself for our sins, that He might deliver us from this present evil world, according to the will of God and our Father." - Galatians 1:4

"He LORD will preserve him, and keep him alive; and he shall be blessed upon the earth: and Thou wilt not deliver him unto the will of his enemies." - Psalms 41:2

"He delivered us from such a deadly peril, and he will deliver us. On him we have set our hope that he will deliver us again." - 2 Corinthians 1:10

"Do not be afraid of them, for I am with you to deliver you, declares the LORD." - Jeremiah 1:8

"I will deliver you out of the hand of the wicked, and redeem you from the grasp of the ruthless." - Jeremiah 15:21

Victory in Jesus

You have victory in Christ through His death, burial, and resurrection, which should cause you to triumph over the enemy, not the other way.

You always have victory through prayer and Jesus.[19]

Below are scriptures highlighting your victory in Jesus:

"Submit yourselves, then, to God. Resist the devil and he will flee from you." -James 4:7

"If the Son sets you free, you will be free indeed." - John 8:36

"And these signs will accompany those who believe: in my name they will cast out demons; they will speak in new tongues." - Mark 16:17

"He has delivered us from the domain of darkness and transferred us to the kingdom of his beloved Son." - Colossians 1:13

"For freedom Christ has set us free; stand firm, therefore, and do not submit again to a yoke of slavery." - Galatians 5:1

"But Jesus rebuked him, saying, "Be silent, and come out of him!" - Mark 1:25

"The seventy returned with joy, saying, "Lord, even the demons are subject to us in Your name." - Luke 10:17

"The Spirit of the Lord is upon me because He has anointed me to preach the gospel to the poor; He has sent me to heal the brokenhearted, to preach deliverance to the captives, and recovering of sight to the blind, to set at liberty them that are bruised, to preach the favorable year of the Lord." - Luke 4:18-19

"But thanks be to God, who gives us the victory through our Lord Jesus Christ!" - 1 Corinthians 15:57

"No, in all these things we are more than conquerors through him who loved us." - Romans 8:37

Authority Over Darkness

Believers have authority over darkness because of Christ. The scriptures below show you how:

"He has rescued us from the dominion of darkness and brought us into the kingdom of the Son he loves." - Colossians 1:13

"They triumphed over him by the blood of the Lamb and by the word of their testimony." - Revelation 12:11

"Behold, I have given you authority to tread on serpents and scorpions, and over all the power of the enemy, and nothing shall hurt you." - Luke 10:19 ESV

"And he called the twelve together and gave them power and authority over all demons and to cure diseases." - Luke 9:1 ESV

"And they were casting out many demons and were anointing with oil many sick people and healing them." - Mark 6:13

"To open their eyes and turn them from darkness to light, and from the power of Satan to God, so that they may receive forgiveness of sins and a place among those who are sanctified by faith in me." - Acts 26:18

"The people living in darkness have seen a great light; on those living in the land of the shadow of death, a light has dawned." - Matthew 4:16

"I saw Satan fall like lightning from heaven." - Luke 10:18

"The night is nearly over; the day is almost here. So let us put aside the deeds of darkness and put on the armor of light." - Romans 13:12

"And this she kept doing for many days. Paul, having become greatly annoyed, turned and said to the spirit, "I command you in the name of Jesus Christ to come out of her." And it came out that very hour." - Acts 16:18

Protection Prayers

Much of what is happening around the world causes you to fear and feel agitated. This feeling often comes from the desire to stay shielded and protected from troubles. Whenever you sense agitation or worry creeping in, take it as a call to prayer. Protection prayers are weapons of faith and spiritual defense that comfort, guide, and assure you of God's protective presence.

Protection prayers to have in your prayer journal are:

Prayer for Personal Protection

You're the most important person in your destiny, so always pray for your well-being.

Scripture: *"The Lord will keep you from all harm—He will watch over your life."* - Psalms 121:7

Prayer: *"Father, I take refuge in You, my shield and protector. Guard my heart, mind, and body from harm. Let no evil come near me, and deliver me from every enemy snare. Cover me under your wings and let Your angels encamp around me. I trust You, and I declare that no weapon formed against me shall prosper. In Jesus' name, Amen."*

Scripture: *"Finally, be strong in the Lord and in His mighty power. Put on the full armor of God, so that you can take your stand against the devil's schemes. For our struggle is not against flesh and blood, but against the rulers, against the authorities, against the powers of this dark world, and against the spiritual forces of evil in the heavenly realms."* - Ephesians 6:10-12 NIV

Prayer: *"Dear Lord, I come to Your refuge with joy, for You shelter me against the devil's attack. Protect me, O Lord, from the enemy's craftiness, and save me from his evil plots."*

Prayer for Protection Over Family

Are you worried about your family and loved ones? You can pray for them in this manner:

Scripture: *"But the Lord is faithful, and He will strengthen you and protect you from the evil one."* - 2 Thessalonians 3:3

Prayer: *"Lord, I lift my family to You. Protect them from all harm, physically and spiritually. Let no scheme of the enemy succeed against them. Surround them with Your angels and guard their hearts and minds in Christ Jesus. May they walk in Your light, and may my home be a place of peace and faith. In Jesus' name, Amen."*

Prayer for Protection Over Home

God's protective hand can be extended to your home. Here's how to pray for this protection:

Scripture: *"Unless the Lord watches over the city, the guards stand watch in vain."* - Psalms 127:1

Prayer: *"Father, I dedicate my home to You. May it be a place of peace, free from fear, darkness, and strife. Let Your presence dwell in every room, filling it with love and unity. Keep every door and window guarded from evil, and let my home be a house of prayer and refuge. In Jesus' name, Amen."*

Prayer for Protection Over Community and Nation

God is particular about every community and nation. You can ask God to preserve both in prayer as follows:

Scripture: *"If My people, who are called by My name, will humble themselves and pray and seek My face and turn from their wicked ways, then I will hear from heaven, and I will forgive their sin and will heal their land."* - 2 Chronicles 7:14

Prayer: *"Lord, I pray for my community and my nation. Heal the land and turn people's hearts back to You. Protect the streets, schools, and leaders. Raise people of faith to shine Your light in dark places. Let righteousness and justice prevail, and may Your will be done in cities and nations. In Jesus' name, Amen."*

Prayer for Protection at Work

Scripture: *"God is our refuge and strength, a very present help in trouble."* - Psalms 46:1

Prayer: *"Father, nothing is impossible for You. I ask for protection at my workplace. Help me to outperform beyond expectations in every task. Thank you for making my boss protective and helpful in assisting me with obtaining job security and appropriate resources. Amen"*

Prayers for Protection While Driving

Here is a simple prayer to say while on the road:

Scripture: *"He will not let your foot be moved; he who keeps you will not slumber."* - Psalms 121:3

Prayer: *"God, by Your mercy, I arrive safely at my destination today. I pray also for the safety of the other drivers I'll share the road with today. Help us to be patient and attentive. Protect us from the dangerous conditions of the vehicles and roads. You're a God of protection who guided and kept the journeys of Abraham and Sarah, and Mary and Joseph safe. Amen"*

Prayer for Protection in Times of Fear

In moments of fear and despair, say this prayer:

Scripture: *"Fear not, for I am with you; be not dismayed, for I am your God; I will strengthen you, I will help you, I will uphold you with my righteous right hand."* - Isaiah 41:10 ESV

Prayer: *"Father, in moments of fear and uncertainty, I turn to You for refuge. Replace my anxiety with Your peace and my fear with trust in Your providence. Help me to remember that You are with me always, and no challenge is too great for me. I declare that I am under Your protection and I find my security in Your unfailing love. In Jesus' name, Amen."*

Prayer for Protection in Spiritual Warfare

Are you currently experiencing the enemy's attack? Here is a prayer:

Scripture: *"Finally, be strong in the Lord and in the strength of his might. Put on the whole armor of God, that you may be able to stand against the schemes of the devil. For we do not wrestle against flesh and blood, but against the rulers, against the authorities, against the cosmic powers over this present darkness, against the spiritual forces of evil in the heavenly places.*

Therefore, take up the whole armor of God, that you may be able to withstand in the evil day, and having done all, to stand firm. Stand therefore, having fastened on the belt of truth, and having put on the

breastplate of righteousness, and, as shoes for your feet, having put on the readiness given by the gospel of peace.

In all circumstances, take up the shield of faith, with which you can extinguish all the flaming darts of the evil one; and take the helmet of salvation, and the sword of the Spirit, which is the Word of God, praying at all times in the Spirit, with all prayer and supplication. To that end, keep alert with all perseverance, making supplication for all the saints." - Ephesians 6:10-18

Prayer: *"Dear Father, I put on the full armor of God to stand against the enemy's schemes. I arm myself with the belt of truth, the breastplate of righteousness, the shoes of the gospel of peace, the shield of faith, the helmet of salvation, and the sword of the Spirit, which is Your Word. I trust in Your strength and protection as I navigate the spiritual battles around me. In Jesus' name, Amen."*

Prayer for Protection Against Temptation

Temptation is evil born from man's nature or the devil. Here is a way to pray against it:

Scriptures: *"Watch and pray, that ye enter not into temptation: the spirit indeed is willing, but the flesh is weak."* - Matthew 26:41

Prayer: *"Dear Father, thank you for revealing how the Lord Jesus overcame temptation by declaring scriptures, and the place of prayer when combating this evil world and its allurements. I ask for the strength and faith to stand firm against this evil world and discernment to recognize when my fleshly desires pull me against Your will. In my fight to avoid sin, help me overcome my daily struggles. Lord, You desire that I be perfect against sin, so lead me not into temptation but deliver me from every appearance of evil. Thank you, Father, in Jesus' name. Amen"*

Prayer of Protection When Traveling

Regardless of your mode of transportation, you need God's protection to reach your destination. Say this prayer when traveling:

Scripture: *"The Lord went before the Israelites in a pillar of cloud by day and a pillar of fire by night to guide them on their journey."* - Exodus 13:21

Prayer: *"Father, as I embark on this journey, I ask for Your protection. Watch over the vehicle [or means of transportation] and keep all passengers safe. Guide the hands of those who operate the* *transportation, and grant me a safe arrival at my destination. I trust in Your traveling mercies and commit this journey into Your hands. In Jesus' name, Amen."*

For a more in-depth study of the topics in this chapter, check out the author's book, Spiritual Warfare (*How to Protect Yourself and Your Loved Ones from Spiritual Attacks, Energy Vampires, Entities, Demons, and Curses*).

Chapter 8: Living Daily in God's Strength

You have everything you need; the Word of God was created to guide you into becoming more in tune with your Creator. When you're aligned with God, you exhibit your full potential. As you study and become more acquainted with the Bible, you discover that it doesn't instruct you to do everything by yourself, nor will God do everything for you. Rather, the Bible deliberately highlights the principle of partnership. It shows you how God will do certain things as a Creator and Father. Then, your job as an earthly partner is to respond to what He does. The power and the resources to live a fulfilled life have been disbursed.

The Word of God, through life and community, will make you stronger.[30]

However, your actions can cause their manifestation or a halt in the process. So, you need light and strength. When the Light of God comes on you, it illuminates your heart, helping you understand your stance in the Spirit. However, it doesn't end there. Even when you have the light, you may not be sufficiently equipped to handle situations without drawing strength. This strength is not physical but spiritual; it's of and from God.

The Spirit of God dwells within you. He becomes a part of you when you are baptized by the Word (accepting Christ as Lord). He is a gift from God (Acts 2:38-41). You receive and are filled with Him when you believe. It's through this Spirit, directly connected to the Divine source - God, that you draw inner strength. It is by this same Spirit that you can boldly proclaim victory in any circumstance:

"But if the Spirit of him that raised Jesus from the dead dwell in you, he that raised up Christ from the dead shall also quicken your mortal bodies by his Spirit that dwelleth in you."- Romans 8:11 KJV

Know that you can only eat fruit from a well-nourished tree, meaning that inasmuch as God supplies you from His never-ending source, you cannot fully enjoy that supply if you do not tend to the channel it comes through. Remember, it's by the Holy Spirit's fellowship that God has called His children to partner with Him. He knows how much you need Him, yet desires your permission to function in you. It's the extent to which you let Him freely flow in you that you experience His Power. The enemy will hide behind situations to obscure your gaze from God, but you must continue to look to Him in faith. As a believer, you must constantly remind yourself that building and maintaining your spiritual strength via your daily habits is expedient.

"Therefore, my dear friends, as you have always obeyed—not only in my presence, but now much more in my absence—continue to work out your salvation with fear and trembling, for it is God who works in you to will and to act in order to fulfill his good purpose." - Philippians 2:12-13

Creating spiritual habits is one way to work out your salvation. These habits consciously remind you of your need for God. The book on Spiritual warfare acquainted you with a consistent prayer life, Bible study, worship, praise, thanksgiving, and complete reliance on God. Living daily in God's strength goes deeper than putting on the whole armor of God. Yes, you can withstand the enemy's fiery darts with the armor's help, but you may be unaware of which tool to wield and when without light. Also, without God's strength, you may be unable to carry these tools into battle. Spiritual warfare isn't only the battles you fight; it's the lifestyle you sustain.

Spiritual Warfare: Maintaining a Godly Lifestyle

Besides helping you defeat your enemies and win battles, God is more interested in your ability to portray Christ's lifestyle. The Bible doesn't specifically instruct you to depend on your strength, nor does it command you to leave it all to God without being involved. God supplies the resources. However, he needs man to maintain and manage those supplies. Hence, leading a godly lifestyle is imperative.

Consider this scenario: in a kingdom, the greatest honor goes to the son who fights in a war. He goes in the name and title of his father, accompanied by his father's armies. On the contrary, there is little to no honor for the son who sits around in the castle, eating, dining, and enjoying the victories of those who fought without partaking in the fight. This applies to every believer - God is a loving Father, yet He gets joy when you share in His Power and live in His Presence.

"I am the vine; you are the branches. If you remain in me and I in you, you will bear much fruit; apart from me, you can do nothing. I have told you this so that my joy may be in you and that your joy may be complete." - John 15:5,11

You build a conviction in His presence of your identity in Him. Hence, the Father is constantly bringing your attention to Him. He matters to you, and you to Him, so He desires that you always share in a sweet fellowship with Him (2 Corinthians 13:14). How do you do this?

Living daily in God's strength begins with a choice. Choose to please Him in everything you do, including the tiniest decisions you make daily. Make it an ambition to become an ambassador of Christ, living a life that portrays His love and grace so others will see and be encouraged.

"We are, therefore, Christ's ambassadors, as though God were making his appeal through us. We implore you on Christ's behalf: Be reconciled to God." - 2 Corinthians 5:20

When Jesus called His disciples, they had jobs, lifestyles, families, and friends, but without hesitation, they forsook all to follow Jesus. No one says that you must quit your job or isolate yourself from everyone. It means that following Jesus comes with a price. Nothing is free. Even salvation was paid for with Christ's blood. There's work to be done daily to enjoy God's strength. When it's difficult to maintain this lifestyle, remember the following scripture and pray with it:

"But those who wait on the Lord Shall renew their strength; They shall mount up with wings like eagles, they shall run and not be weary, they shall walk and not faint." - Isaiah 40:31 NKJV

Why Consistency Matters

Consistency has always been the key to building a successful life. A lifestyle is formed via consistent habits, and habits are formed from routines. Habits are routines you've practiced frequently and register in your subconscious, and they are difficult to stop. When you engage in activities consistently, the results give you fulfillment. For example, when people hit the gym, they often have one goal: to lose weight or build body muscle. At first, it appears as a mere desire or wish. Nothing usually happens in the first few days of this engagement. What accompanies the newfound commitment are soreness and body aches. If they look beyond the pain and continue, in a few weeks, they'll see little changes. This joy in seeing the result of their work stirs up a strong commitment to continue. Why? Because they believe that with these little results, they can attain their goal within a set time.

This explanation isn't for physical demonstrations alone. It also works for spiritual goals. Daily activities like prayer, worship, Bible study, meditation, and thanksgiving build your spiritual muscle. You can be trusted with higher manifestations when consistently committing to these habits. You cannot lift heavy weights without consistently lifting lighter ones. It's the lighter weights that build the muscles for the heavier ones.

Daily Habits to Build Spiritual Strength

Set up a spiritual routine to build spiritual strength; this requires commitment and a conscious effort. Naturally, your flesh doesn't desire to engage in activities of the spirit, and vice versa, as explained in the previous chapter. However, you have the Holy Spirit's help to live above the weakness of the flesh.

"But he said to me, "My grace is sufficient for you, for my power is made perfect in weakness." Therefore, I will boast all the more gladly about my weaknesses, so that Christ's power may rest on me." - 2 Corinthians 12:9 NIV

Initially, you won't have it all figured out. However, no matter how little you begin with, strive to be consistent. Consistently accomplishing five minutes of prayer to kickstart each day goes a long way than doing 3 hours and being unable to keep it up in the following weeks.

Here's a breakdown of daily habits to build spiritual strength:

Morning Prayer and Faith Journaling

Morning prayer is a good way to begin your day; it sets the tone for your entire day. A simple prayer in the morning will keep your consciousness of God alert throughout the day. Also, it helps you think about your day and open your mind only to God's will for the day. Set a time for God in the morning's early hours; this exercise is wholesome. God enjoys fellowshipping with His Children, so you can be sure of the blessing of His presence. An example of God's love for fellowshipping with you is in the beginning when God came to the Garden of Eden to fellowship with Adam in the cool of the day. You can also see that Jesus maintained this practice throughout His time on Earth.

"Very early in the morning, while it was still dark, Jesus got up, left the house, and went off to a solitary place, where he prayed." - Mark 1:35

At first, your prayers don't need to last for hours – start small by giving a few minutes each morning to prayer. All that matters to God is the sincerity of your prayers. Begin with a simple prayer like this:

"Lord, as I begin this day, I invite You to lead my steps. Let my heart be sensitive to Your voice, and help me walk in faith and obedience. Strengthen me against distractions and temptations, and fill me with Your peace. In Jesus' name, Amen."

As you pray, prepare your heart in faith. God speaks, and soon, your ears will be open to hear Him audibly. Have your journal with you as you present yourself to God to prepare by faith. Missing what God says due to a lack of journaling is a painful experience, so don't go to God without being prepared. Also, jot down your visions and dreams and pray for interpretation, as well as your questions, needs, and worries to pray for direction and answers. Whenever you pray sincerely, God always hears you. However, manifesting His answer might need patience, persistent faith, and hope; they will come eventually.

"And without faith, it is impossible to please God, because anyone who comes to him must believe that he exists and that he rewards those who earnestly seek him." - Hebrews 11:6

Daily Scripture Reading and Meditation

A few minutes of intentional reading and deliberate meditation on God's Word daily will bring you into the Spirit's Divine wisdom. Reading can seem ordinary until meditation through prayer is practiced. Reading the Bible helps you get familiar with God's promises, studying enables you to get acquainted, and meditation helps you become a reality of those words. Remember, the Word of God is living and active and discerns the heart's intentions (Hebrews 4:12). It's powerful enough to transform anyone from within.

A few minutes of intentional reading and meditation go a long way.[31]

"Keep this Book of the Law always on your lips; meditate on it day and night so that you may be careful to do everything written in it. Then you will be prosperous and successful." -Joshua 1:8

Begin with a Psalm and a chapter from any gospel (preferably John), or go online for a realistic Bible reading plan. Whatever scriptures stand out to you as you read, stop, highlight them, and write them out. When you're done reading, repeat the verse to yourself over and over again, as you would a memory verse. Search the Greek or Hebrew meaning of vague or generic words for better context. Find out if the words are portrayed as nouns, verbs, singular, or plural tense. Have a journal where you jot down your observations. After each study, ask the Holy Ghost (the author of the scriptures) to bring to your understanding what He wants you to learn or know from the scriptures. Pray the scripture until your understanding of it becomes illuminated. Ask Him to help you apply the wisdom of the Word in your life daily. Be open to hearing Him, because He speaks.

Worship and Thanksgiving

The book on Spiritual Warfare explains that Worship is more than a song; it's a posture of the heart, a sacrifice, and your reasonable service unto God.

"Therefore, I urge you, brothers and sisters, in view of God's mercy, to offer your bodies as a living sacrifice, holy and pleasing to God—this is your true and proper worship." - Romans 12:1

Worship is done in and out of good times and seasons, making it a sacrifice. Worship can be made to God via thanksgiving, acts of service, songs and hymns, prayer, confessions, a broken heart, obedience to God's word, preaching the gospel, or giving to the needy. However, this chapter focuses on worshiping God through thanksgiving and songs.

- **Thanksgiving:** Each morning or before you lie in bed for the day, write out 5 things you're grateful to God for. Think about your day for a notable experience of God coming through for you or a lesson you received from Him. This shifts your attention from complaining to viewing the world as God sees it.

- **Songs and Hymns:** It's okay if you're unfamiliar with many hymns and worship songs. Often, people struggle to make sense of several songs at once, so even a lyric by heart is perfect. Understand the song and sing its lyrics like you are conversing with God. The book of Psalms is littered with songs sung from a man's heart to God. Many of David's songs are conversations with God. These songs express David's heart at different times - praises, painful expressions, seeking deliverance, asking for mercy, and acknowledging God's awesomeness. Express your heart to God at any time in hymns and songs. When you're in a situation, lift a song to God (you could form the lyrics yourself) as a form of worship. God isn't searching for a perfect voice.

"Sing to the Lord a new song; sing to the Lord, all the earth. Sing to the Lord, praise his name; proclaim his salvation day after day." - Psalms 96:1-2

Praying Through the Day

Praying is an art because it can take any form. Who says prayer can only be when you're on your knees and fold your hands together, resting them on your temple? Breathing out your prayer is considered a prayer posture or form. It doesn't mean you have to breathe out fire like a dragon. It can be muttering words under your breath as you go about your daily activities. There are many techniques for praying. You do not have to apply them all *every time*, but you must equip yourself with knowledge and understanding through practice.

"*Rejoice evermore. Pray without ceasing. In everything give thanks: for this is the will of God in Christ Jesus concerning you.*" - 1 Thessalonians 5:16-18

Now, to make it practical:

- You're having a bad day? Immediately pray under your breath
- Do you suddenly feel tense before a presentation? Pray under your breath
- Do you need directions in a confusing situation? Pray under your breath
- Do you need help with something? Pray
- Do you suddenly feel weak and need strength? Pray under your breath
- You don't know what or how to answer in a conversation? Pray under your breath
- Before sleeping? Pray
- Do you remember God's goodness? Pray
- You receive news - good or unpleasant? pray

The list is endless. Apostle Paul says that since the issues never cease, neither should your prayers.

Here are prayers to kick-start your journey of daily living in God's strength:

Prayer for Strength in Hard Times: "*Lord, I surrender my struggles to You. Give me the strength to face each challenge with faith and courage. Remind me that You are always in control, and Your grace is sufficient for me. I trust You to provide all I need today. In Jesus' name, Amen.*"

Nighttime Prayer: *"Father, I give this day to You. Thank you for guiding me, protecting me, and strengthening me. Forgive my shortcomings and fill my heart with peace as I rest. I trust You with tomorrow. In Jesus' name, Amen."*

Daily Prayer for Walking in the Light of Christ: *"Heavenly Father, thank you for calling me out of darkness into Your marvelous light. Help me to walk in the light of Your truth each day. Guide my steps, fill me with Your Spirit, and protect me from the enemy's schemes. Let my life reflect Your love and bring glory to Your name. Strengthen me to be a light to others and share Christ's hope wherever I go. In Jesus' name. Amen."*

Living daily in God's strength isn't a lofty life preserved for only a "special set of individuals." It's a normal life that God invites His children into. It begins with simple, intended habits: morning prayers, faith journaling, Bible study, meditation, worship, thanksgiving, and continuous learning at His feet. It's sustained by God's strength, for without Him, you can do nothing of your own. God isn't looking for perfection. He searches for a heart that seeks and lusts after Him. Whether it's a short prayer whispered in weakness or a song sung in imperfection, it doesn't matter. What matters is that as you engage in these, you draw nigh to His strength and fall right into His loving embrace. Consistency may seem shaky initially, but press on, and over time, it becomes a part of you, and your life will be anchored in grace, power, wisdom, peace, and the Love of God. As you commit to walking with Him daily, you're constantly being renewed, straightened, and transformed from within. Zechariah 4:6b says, *"Not by your might, nor by your power, but by His Spirit."* Let today be the start of a new and higher life for you.

Conclusion

You'll agree that this has been a journey, and kudos to you for seeing it through. Now, the work begins, and the doer of the work accompanying this Spiritual Warfare Prayers companion sees results.

Spiritual Warfare comes to the believer in many forms - spiritual, emotional, physical, or psychological. When the enemy attacks, he doesn't want you to know he's behind it. He thrives by keeping you in the dark, and when you're unaware of his moves or your victory in Christ, you can't truly fight or know the right tools to use. The Bible states clearly that the enemy is crafty and uses many devices (deception, temptation, fear, lies, etc.). You must not be ignorant of his devices. Hence, this book is perfect for combating the enemy's lies and walking in Christ's victory.

The principles from this book were not given to fill your head but to change your life, and a changed life can only happen when you actively put on the armor of God and engage in prayers of strength, protection, and deliverance. Declare aloud to yourself the Bible verses that speak about your victory and authority in Christ, and maintain a daily habit of prayers, Bible reading, worship, gratitude, and total reliance on God.

The principles shared in this book are timeless; they are weapons against the enemy in your time of spiritual darkness, emphasizing God's Word. Since dark times will never cease in this world, you shouldn't relent in falling back on this book from time to time.

As believers, Christ's power and victory have been given to you to use and enjoy. Your position is not to champion a new course or defeat the devil to obtain victory because Christ has already done that. You have been called to maintain the authority to stand in Christ's victory, seeing it as your victory, and to make war from the place of victory, not striving for victory. It's remarkable how you have been put over and above by Christ, and this spiritual warfare prayer book was written to ensure you stay committed.

Now, go and live the life Christ has called you to live. Grace to your heart. Amen!

If you enjoyed this book, I'd greatly appreciate a review on Amazon because it helps me to create more books that people want. It would mean a lot to hear from you.

To leave a review:
1. Open your camera app.
2. Point your mobile device at the QR code.
3. The review page will appear in your web browser.

Thanks for your support!

Here's another book by Mari Silva that you might like

Your Free Gift
(only available for a limited time)

Thanks for getting this book! If you want to learn more about various spirituality topics, then join Mari Silva's community and get a free guided meditation MP3 for awakening your third eye. This guided meditation mp3 is designed to open and strengthen ones third eye so you can experience a higher state of consciousness. Simply visit the link below the image to get started.

https://spiritualityspot.com/meditation
Or, Scan the QR code!

References

3 Things You Need to Know About Taking Authority Over Satan. (2025). Karenjensen.org. https://karenjensen.org/media-menu/blog/1602-3-things-you-need-to-know-about-taking-authority-over-satan

4 of Satan's Best Strategies and How to Resist Them. (2019). Churchofjesuschrist.org. https://www.churchofjesuschrist.org/study/ya-weekly/2019/11/4-of-satans-best-strategies-and-how-to-resist-them?lang=eng

Blossom, A. (2021, October 19). *The Tactics of Satan - Fear & Doubt.* All Things Life. https://www.allthingslife.org/post/the-tactics-of-satan-fear-doubt

Jana. (2023, August 14). *Bible Study Tips for Beginners: How to Study the Bible in Context | Jana Carlson.* Jana Carlson. https://janacarlson.com/bible-study-tips-for-beginners-how-to-study-the-bible-in-context/

Lifeway Women. (2015, June 9). *How Do We Pray God's Word? - Lifeway Women.* Lifeway Women. https://women.lifeway.com/2015/06/09/pray-gods-word/

Raveling, B. (2021, March 24). *How to Meditate on Scripture - A Beginner's Guide.* Barb Raveling. https://barbraveling.com/how-to-meditate-on-scripture/

Spiritual Warfare and Fasting – John 9:14-29. (2017, April 2). CHRIST ALLIANCE CHURCH. https://christalliance.org/2017/04/02/spiritual-warfare-and-fasting-john-914-29/

Spiritual Warfare: Understanding Satan's Strategies. (n.d.). Biblestudytools.com. https://www.biblestudytools.com/bible-study/topical-studies/spiritual-warfare-lesson-2-the-strategies-of-satan-11580094.html

Swearingen, S. (2021, February 1). *Spiritual Warfare: Definition, Viewpoints, and Why it Matters.* Just Disciple. https://justdisciple.com/spiritual-warfare/

Love. (2015). Praying the Armor of God: Trusting God to Protect You and the People You Love. Logos.com. https://www.logos.com/product/52114/praying-the-armor-of-god-trusting-god-to-protect-you-and-the-people-you-love

ed. (2016). A Prayer Warrior's Guide to Spiritual Battle: The Front Line, 2nd ed. Lexhampress.com. https://lexhampress.com/product/72603/a-prayer-warriors-guide-to-spiritual-battle-the-front-line-2nd-ed

Kennard, E., Adejuwon, E., & Conway, X. (2020). Sword Prayers: Full Armor of God Warfare Prayers to Defeat the Enemy! Goodreads. https://www.goodreads.com/en/book/show/55279757-sword-prayers

Staff, B. (2021, August 30). *The Full Armor of God: How to Pray - Billy Graham Training Center at the Cove.* Billy Graham Training Center at the Cove. https://thecove.org/blog/the-full-armor-of-god-how-to-pray/

Debbie. (2016, August 14). Praying on the Armor of God. Debbie McDaniel. https://debbiemcdaniel.com/2016/08/14/praying-armor-god/

Bible, N.I.V. (2018, June 3). 10 bible verses on strength. NIV Bible. https://www.thenivbible.com/blog/inspiring-bible-verses/

Topical bible: Understanding spiritual darkness. (n.d.). Biblehub.com. https://biblehub.com/topical/u/understanding_spiritual_darkness.htm

What is prayer? (2016, March 24). Gotquestions.org. https://www.gotquestions.org/what-is-prayer.html

Gahm, V. (2024, May 27). *How to Pray Specific Scriptures Over Your Circumstances.* Boundless. https://www.boundless.org/faith/how-to-pray-specific-scriptures-over-your-circumstances/

God's Word Is A Weapon. (2024). Leesburg Christian Church. https://www.leesburgchristianchurch.net/blog/2024/02/26/god-s-word-is-a-weapon

How to Win Daily Battles of the Mind. (2025). Https://Joycemeyer.org/Grow-Your-Faith/Articles/How-To-Win-Daily-Battles-of-The-Mind. https://joycemeyer.org/Grow-Your-Faith/Articles/How-to-Win-Daily-Battles-of-the-Mind

Jack Graham - Declare Your Victory» Watch Online Sermons 2025. (2025). Watch Online Sermons 2025. https://sermons.love/jack-graham/12730-jack-graham-declare-your-victory.html#google_vignette

Lifeway Women. (2015, June 9). *How Do We Pray God's Word? - Lifeway Women.* Lifeway Women. https://women.lifeway.com/2015/06/09/pray-gods-word/

Perez, K. (2021, August). *How to Pray Scripture.* The Daily Grace Co. https://thedailygraceco.com/blogs/the-daily-grace-blog/how-to-pray-scripture

Harcourt, F. (2021, June 26). *How To Maintain Our Victory - Felix Harcourt Ministries*. Felix Harcourt Ministries. https://www.fhmi.net/how-to-maintain-our-victory/

https://www.facebook.com/thejamestaiwo. (2021, June 5). Book of Prayers - Inspirational Quotes & Articles. Inspirational Quotes & Articles. https://jamestaiwo.com/book-of-prayers/

Tammie. (2021, June 7). The 10 Best Books on Prayer - Life, Love, and Jesus. Life, Love, and Jesus. https://www.lifeloveandjesus.com/the-10-best-books-on-prayer/

Seed, H. (2023, August 8). 27 Great Books on Prayer for Pastors to Read and Recommend - PastorMentor. PastorMentor. https://pastormentor.com/books-on-prayer/

Wise, J. (2015, June 11). A Collection of Prayers and Quotes about Prayer. Healthy Spirituality. https://healthyspirituality.org/a-collection-of-prayers-and-quotes-about-prayer/

Fast, D. (2023, November 7). Daniel Fast Journey. Daniel Fast Journey. https://www.danielfastjourney.com/blog/quotes-about-fasting-and-prayer-for-christians

Ingram, C. (2021, June 14). 12 Powerful Scriptures For Spiritual Warfare Resistance. Living on the Edge. https://livingontheedge.org/2021/06/14/powerful-scriptures-for-spiritual-warfare/

Jordan, R. B. (2021, March 8). Spiritual Warfare Prayer for Supernatural Help in the Battle. Crosswalk.com; Crosswalk. https://www.crosswalk.com/faith/prayer/a-prayer-for-spiritual-warfare.html

Savchuk, V. (2023, August 7). 30 Declarations to Break the Spirit of Fear. Vladimir Savchuk Ministries. https://pastorvlad.org/againstfear/

McDaniel, D. (2023, April 4). 31 Spiritual Warfare Scriptures: Help for Facing Life's Battles. Crosswalk.com; Crosswalk. https://www.crosswalk.com/faith/spiritual-life/31-spiritual-warfare-scriptures.html

Trimm, C. (2021, June 23). DTP. DTP. https://successfulservantleader.com/blog/warfareprayer

Coren. (2024, February 9). *What is a Stronghold? – Catching Courage*. Catching Courage. https://catchingcourage.blog/what-is-a-stronghold/

Forbes, R. (2024, May 14). *Daily Devotionals by Rich Forbes*. Daily Devotionals by Rich Forbes. https://richinpraise.com/devotionals/2024/5/14/praying-against-temptation

Lehigh University. (n.d.). Www1.Lehigh.edu. https://www.lehigh.edu/

Powerful Prayers for Protection from Evil and Physical Harm. (n.d.). Christianity.com. https://www.christianity.com/wiki/prayer/prayers-for-protection-pray-for-safety.html

Praying for Deliverance and Protection. (2021). Christian Healing Ministries. https://www.christianhealingmin.org/index.php?option=com_content&view=article&id=1207:praying-for-deliverance-and-protection&catid=295&Itemid=101

Promises for: Deliverance in the LORD. (2025). Whatsaiththescripture.com. https://www.whatsaiththescripture.com/Promises/Promises.Deliverance.html

Savchuk, V. (2021, June 21). *8 Steps To Be Self-Delivered.* Vladimir Savchuk Ministries. https://pastorvlad.org/howtobeselfdelivered/

Spiewak, S. (2024, August 16). *Prayers for Protection: Praying for Safety from Evil and Danger.* Hallow. https://hallow.com/blog/prayers-for-protection/#driving

Staff, E. (2020, February 20). *25 Powerful Prayers for Protection and Safety.* Crosswalk.com; Crosswalk. https://www.crosswalk.com/faith/prayer/5-powerful-prayers-for-protection.html

Understanding God's Protection in the Christian Faith. (2023). Wisdom International. https://www.wisdomonline.org/blog/protection/

What Does the Bible Say About All Power And Authority Over The Devil? (2025). Openbible.info. https://www.openbible.info/topics/all_power_and_authority_over_the_devil

What Does the Bible Say About Delivered From The Powers Of Darkness? (2025). Openbible.info. https://www.openbible.info/topics/delivered_from_the_powers_of_darkness

Crossway, B. (2023, March 21). 10 key bible verses on baptism. Crossway. https://www.crossway.org/articles/10-key-bible-verses-on-baptism/?srsltid=AfmBOorD5tbSRDdoK979LmlVTWD65UwF9WA6PRZErsRo0R_vtOF8FIzI

McLachlan, S. (2021, December 22). The science of habit. Healthline; Healthline Media. https://www.healthline.com/health/the-science-of-habit

Image Sources

1 Phillip Medhurst, CC BY-SA 3.0 <https://creativecommons.org/licenses/by-sa/3.0/>, via Wikimedia Commons https://commons.wikimedia.org/wiki/File:Apocalypse_8._Opening_the_seals._Revelation_cap_8_v_1-5._Mortier%27s_Bible._Phillip_Medhurst_Collection.jpg

2 I, Luc Viatour, CC BY-SA 3.0 <http://creativecommons.org/licenses/by-sa/3.0/>, via Wikimedia Commons https://commons.wikimedia.org/wiki/File:Lucifer_Liege_Luc_Viatour_new.jpg

3 Photo by Jack Sharp on Unsplash https://unsplash.com/photos/man-praying-OptEsFuZwoQ

4 Photo by Ricardo Cruz on Unsplash https://unsplash.com/photos/close-up-photography-of-gold-colored-and-black-sword-DCqvWkXF74Q

5 Photo by Rod Long on Unsplash https://unsplash.com/photos/persons-hand-holding-book-page-DRgrzQQsJDA

6 Claudia Thunnissen, CC BY 4.0 <https://creativecommons.org/licenses/by/4.0>, via Wikimedia Commons https://commons.wikimedia.org/wiki/File:Cingulum_riem_Romeinse_soldaat_20160410_fotoCThunnissen.jpg

7 Rept0n1x, CC BY-SA 3.0 <https://creativecommons.org/licenses/by-sa/3.0/>, via Wikimedia Commons https://commons.wikimedia.org/wiki/File:Replica_armour_of_a_Roman_legionary,_Worcester_City_Art_Gallery_%26_Museum,_England_-_DSCF0766.JPG

8 Carole Raddato from FRANKFURT, Germany, CC BY-SA 2.0 <https://creativecommons.org/licenses/by-sa/2.0>, via Wikimedia Commons https://commons.wikimedia.org/wiki/File:Caliga,_Roman_soldiers_sandal_from_the_1st_Century_AD,_Landesmuseum,_Mainz_(11408265805).jpg

9 George E. Koronaios, CC BY-SA 4.0 <https://creativecommons.org/licenses/by-sa/4.0>, via Wikimedia Commons https://commons.wikimedia.org/wiki/File:Roman_shield_(Scutum)_replica_at_Athens_War_Museum_on_November_22,_2022.jpg

10 Hans Splinter, Attribution-NoDerivs 2.0 Generic, CC BY-ND 2.0 < https://creativecommons.org/licenses/by-nd/2.0/deed.en> https://www.flickr.com/photos/archeon/1203437601

11 Photo by Aaron Burden on Unsplash https://unsplash.com/photos/silhouette-of-kneeling-man-lPCu8HnGU2E

12 National Gallery of Art, CC0, via Wikimedia Commons https://commons.wikimedia.org/wiki/File:Giovanni_Girolamo_Savoldo%2C_Elijah_Fed_by_the_Raven%2C_c._1510%2C_NGA_46134_%28cropped%29.jpg

13 Photo by Rodolfo Clix: https://www.pexels.com/photo/close-up-photograph-of-person-praying-in-front-lined-candles-1024900/ https://www.pexels.com/photo/close-up-photograph-of-person-praying-in-front-lined-candles-1024900/

14 Photo by Ric Rodrigues: https://www.pexels.com/photo/man-tattooed-praying-1278566/

15 Photo by Pixabay: https://www.pexels.com/photo/holy-bible-on-stand-372326/

16 Photo by cottonbro studio: https://www.pexels.com/photo/a-woman-in-black-long-sleeve-shirt-sitting-on-wooden-pew-6284305/

17 Photo by Luis Quintero: https://www.pexels.com/photo/grayscale-photography-of-hands-waving-2014773/

18 Photo by Karola G: https://www.pexels.com/photo/close-up-shot-of-a-person-holding-a-rosary-5206837/

19 Photo by Pixabay: https://www.pexels.com/photo/crucifix-illustration-208216/

20 Photo by RDNE Stock project: https://www.pexels.com/photo/women-having-a-conversation-5874911/

21 Photo by Eduardo Braga: https://www.pexels.com/photo/person-holding-opened-book-1296720/

www.ingramcontent.com/pod-product-compliance
Lightning Source LLC
Chambersburg PA
CBHW051843160426